MULTI-DIMENSIONAL INTELLIGENCE:

Activating A Higher Blueprint for Human Evolution

CAROL TALBOT, PhD

GULF BOOK
SERVICES

Published by Gulf Book Services Ltd

20-22 Wenlock Road, London,N1 7GU, UK

Email: info@gulfbooks.co.uk

Office No: G23,

GULF BOOK SERVICES — Sharjah Publishing City Freezone

Sharjah – UAE

First Published by Gulf Book Services Ltd

ISBN: 978-1-917529-29-7

Year: October 2025

In this critical book, Dr Carol Talbot does a fabulous job in connecting many dots in the fields of frequency, resonance, coherence, and consciousness that transcend the physical into the spiritual and etheric realities. She opens our minds to our infinite potential as human beings and brings us closer to a deeper comprehension of our place in an interconnected universe, highlighting our shortfalls and our powers. Once we realize that everything in creation is connected, we will realize our own true potential and hopefully use it wisely. This is a critical book in the rapidly expanding fields of spiritual sciences, where mainstream science meets spirituality.

Michael Tellinger - Founder ONE SMALL TOWN Initiative

An impressive contribution to the field of intelligences. Multi-Dimensional Intelligence provides a much needed and profound exploration of the nature of intelligence, taking the reader way beyond the usual understandings of intelligence into enticing and exciting new realms. Dr Talbot provides an invaluable and impressive overview of current understandings including IQ, EQ and SQ, as well as sharing her powerful innovative multi-dimensional perspective. She calls her book a "doorway," an "activation beyond the veil of the ordinary," and so it is. As a leader and teacher, I have explored different intelligences over many years and was delighted to discover Carol's work. She provides a radical and fascinating challenge to conventional understandings of intelligence and expands the current discourse on artificial intelligence. Most importantly Dr Talbot offers her compelling vision of a radical development and expansion of human intelligence, potential and possibilities.

Dr Lynne Sedgmore CBE - Author of Goddess Luminary Leadership Wheel, and Presence Activism. Coach, Poet, retired Chief Executive and non-executive.

Multi-Dimensional Intelligence is nothing short of revolutionary. Dr. Carol Talbot masterfully bridges quantum science, ancient wisdom, and consciousness exploration to reveal a new framework for human potential and one that redefines intelligence not as data or achievement, but as resonance and frequency. This book is far more than words on a page; it is a transmission, an activation, and a guide to remembering the multi-dimensional being you truly are. If you are ready to awaken latent capacities, expand beyond linear limits, and embody your highest intelligence, this is the book you've been waiting for.

Debbi Dachinger - Award-winning podcast host of Dare to Dream, Shamanic energy Healer, and bestselling author

Dr. Carol Talbot's Multi-Dimensional Intelligence is a powerful transmission for our times. More than a book, it is a frequency key that unlocks the deeper codes of who we are as energetic, multi-dimensional beings. With extraordinary clarity and depth, Carol offers readers a pathway to activate their DNA, expand their perception, and embody their highest potential.
As someone who has worked for decades with energy, space, and consciousness, I deeply resonate with her message: that true intelligence is not just of the mind, but of frequency, coherence, and resonance. This book is a gift for transformational leaders, seekers, and pioneers of the new paradigm. It reminds us that we are navigating reality as well as shaping it.
I highly recommend this book to all who are ready to remember who they truly are and step fully into their radiant power.

Marie Diamond - Global Best-Selling Author, Renowned Feng Shui & Manifestation Master featured in The Secret

This book is a remembering. As a shaman who walks between worlds and listens to what most have forgotten how to hear, I felt this work vibrating in my bones. Multi-Dimensional Intelligence is the language of the soul encoded in frequency. Dr. Carol Talbot is not merely offering ideas; she's revealing the keys to our original design. If you've ever sensed that you are more than flesh, more than thought, and more than time, this book is the map back to your multi-dimensional self.

John Paul EagleHeart - Shaman, Site-Whisperer, Author and Creator/Host of "Spirit Encounters"

The world is more complex and confusing than it's ever been, with the advent of new technologies, new scientific understandings, and the meta crisis of climate change, political polarization, and disinformation. Fortunately, as Carol Talbot informs us, humans are designed to not only respond to this complexity and chaos but also to become creators of a new, more harmonious and resonant era that serves all of life. Weaving science, wisdom and a new understanding of multi-dimensional intelligence, this book provides the theory and practice for finding our unique contributions to making the world a better place. We need multi-dimensional intelligence now more than ever. Put this book on the top of your reading pile!

Judi Neal, Ph.D. - Author, Edgewalkers, Creating Enlightened Organizations, and Inspiring Workplace Spirituality, President, Edgewalkers International Network, www.edgewalkers.org

DEDICATION

To the ones who feel time bends around their choices...
To the quiet rebels who see through the illusion and know there is more...
This book is for you.
For the explorers of inner space...
May you trust the signals that come not from the mind, but from the field.
May you learn to read the language of frequency, of resonance, of
alignment.
For the architects of the unseen...
May you reclaim the codes within your DNA and awaken the intelligence
that was never lost, only waiting for your attention to remember.
For the timeline shifters, the system disruptors, the edge-walkers...
May you anchor coherence where there is chaos, presence where there is
noise,
and hold the blueprint of what is possible when you live multi-dimensionally.
For the ones who came here to transmit...
May you embody the truth that you are not here to follow the map,
you are here to become the compass.
And for the future humans already encoded in your being...
May this work guide your remembrance, activate your mastery,
and awaken the signal that calls others home to themselves

Contents

INTRODUCTION

Beyond the Veil: A New Intelligence Awakens

There are moments in life where reality seems to glitch. You walk into a room, certain you've never been there before, yet every detail feels familiar. You think of someone, and they call within seconds. You dream of an event only to witness it unfold days later. For a moment, logic wavers. A crack forms in the structure of the known world. And something deep inside you whispers: *There is more.*

What if these are glimpses into a greater intelligence, and one that transcends the linear mind, the five senses, and the rigid framework of your conditioned reality? What if intelligence itself is not what you have been led to believe?

For centuries, mankind sought answers in the realms of science, philosophy, and spirituality, searching for the elusive thread that connects the seen and unseen, the logical and the mystical, the known and the ineffable. Some have glimpsed this deeper intelligence in moments of inspiration, déjà vu, or inexplicable knowing. Others have dismissed it as fantasy, the stuff of myths and science fiction. And yet, throughout history, there have been those who dared to peer beyond the veil, who sensed that there was more.

Intelligence has been confined to what is the measurable, the logical, the analytical and the intellectual. But what if intelligence extends beyond IQ, beyond pattern recognition, beyond the very boundaries of space and time? What if it is a field, a force, a living, breathing consciousness that you are designed to tap into?

As a seeker and searcher, endlessly curious about the nature of reality and drawn to the unexplored edges of human potential, my journey has led me down blind alleys, through systems of thought that promised truth but delivered only fragments. Yet, every dead-end whispered the same secret: *You are not who you think you are.*

For years, I sought answers in the usual places, from education and mainstream research to ancient teachings, only to discover that intelligence is not confined to the intellect, nor is reality bound by the rigid walls of logic. The missing key was always there, hidden in plain sight: you are far more than a physical being navigating a linear world; you are multi-dimensional intelligence in motion.

You stand at the threshold of an evolutionary leap, and one that challenges everything you think you know about who you are and what you are capable of. The future of intelligence is not artificial; it is multi-dimensional. It is the ability to perceive beyond the five senses, attune to the unseen forces shaping your reality, and remember the inherent wisdom encoded within you.

You are a multi-dimensional being navigating a world that has been stripped of its magic, a world where children are taught to see only in two dimensions when, in truth, you exist across infinite layers of reality. And now, as the world hurtles toward rapid transformation, the call to awaken your Multi-Dimensional Intelligence has never been louder.

This book is a doorway. An activation. A disruption to everything you once believed about intelligence, reality, and the very nature of who you are.

If you have ever felt that pull and sensed that there is something beyond the veil of the ordinary, then you are already at the threshold.

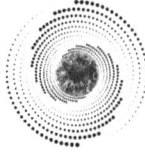

Chapter One

The Evolution of Intelligence: Beyond IQ, EQ & SQ

Introduction
What Does It Mean to Be Intelligent?

Do you consider yourself intelligent?

For most people, the answer to that question is rooted in their experience of formal education. From the moment you step into the structured environment of school, you're placed on a path designed to measure and categorize your intelligence. You're given a curriculum, a script, a set of beliefs, and are filled with facts, figures, and a carefully curated history that may or may not be true. You're trained to memorize, regurgitate, and perform. If you excel at repeating the prescribed information, you're awarded gold stars, top grades, and the esteemed label of being "intelligent." If you struggle or deviate from the script, you're relegated to the sidelines, told to work harder, conform more, and think less abstractly.

But is this true intelligence, or merely conditioning?

As for myself, I never considered myself "intelligent" by conventional standards. I certainly wasn't a star student, nor did I shine academically in a way that was deemed exceptional. I was a moderate pupil, uninterested in the rigid pathways laid out before me. I never pursued university, not because I lacked the ability, but because I never felt drawn to a particular predefined approach to a subject. Looking back, I am profoundly grateful that I did not follow the conventional academic route. Instead, my search for knowledge, wisdom, and understanding took me across the globe, immersing myself in experiences that a traditional education could never have provided.

My classroom became the world and beyond. My teachers were remarkable masters and mentors, and my curriculum encompassed a vast array of sciences, philosophies, and practices that reshaped my perception of reality. I hold a PhD in Quantum Morphogenetic Physics from an unorthodox institution, rooted in the eternal life sciences and an expansive field of knowledge that explores our multi-dimensional design, our true cosmic history, and the hidden layers of our existence.

Mainstream education does not teach you this. Instead, it reduces intelligence to measurable outputs such as test scores, degrees, and standardized assessments, while disregarding the vast potential of expanded perception, creative genius, and intuitive knowing.

Intelligence is not a singular quality. It is not just about intellectual prowess or emotional awareness. Today, many forms of intelligence are spoken about: Intellectual (IQ), Emotional (EQ), Spiritual (SQ), and even Artificial Intelligence (AI). What if there is something beyond all of these?

True intelligence isn't rooted in memorization, but rather in access. It's not about accumulation, but activation. It's the ability to perceive beyond what is visible, to understand beyond what is taught, and to know beyond what is said.

This chapter explores the evolution of intelligence from IQ and standardized metrics to EQ and the intelligence of the heart, from SQ and the wisdom of intuition to Howard Gardner's Multiple Intelligences, all of which prove that intelligence is far more diverse than you may have been led to believe.

Above and beyond learning, true intelligence is about becoming more.

KEY QUESTIONS FOR EXPLORATION IN CHAPTER ONE

◊   Have you ever felt intelligent in ways that couldn't be measured by tests, grades, or formal education?

◊   What if true intelligence is something you remember and reawaken?

◊   Could there be a form of intelligence that transcends logic, emotion, and even spirituality?

Breaking Free from the Old Paradigm

Imagine waking up one morning to find that the world has changed. In this new world, intelligence is no longer measured by IQ tests, academic degrees, or report cards. It's recognized through your capacity to perceive beyond logic, sense beyond the five physical senses, and access a deeper, inner knowing. In this world, value is placed on awareness, intuition, and multi-dimensional perception.

For generations, you've been taught that intelligence must be earned, measured, and validated by external systems. Yet this view is incomplete. Intelligence isn't merely stored in textbooks or machines; it is a frequency, a state of consciousness that lies dormant within you, waiting to be activated.

The rigid structures of schooling, corporate hierarchies, and social expectations have conditioned you to believe that intelligence exists only within defined boundaries. However, true intelligence is expansive. It includes your ability to access heightened awareness, expanded perception, and even interact with the unseen dimensions of reality.

Close your eyes for a moment. Sense what it might feel like to see beyond what your eyes show you, to hear beyond physical sound, and to know without needing proof. Picture a world where knowledge flows effortlessly through you, where thoughts are shared without speaking words, and reality bends in response to your intention.

This isn't fantasy; it's the awakening of what is already within you. This is not just an idea or a possibility. I have experienced it firsthand.

Beyond Sight: The Darkroom Experience

There is something profound that happens when you remove all external stimulation and sit in complete and utter darkness for days, detached from the rhythms of daily life, from the distractions of technology, and even from the conditioned way you've learned to perceive reality.

In 2023, I immersed myself in a darkroom experience at Mantak Chia's purpose-built facility in Northern Thailand. This was a 9-day, 9-night experience that also offered the opportunity to switch to Source Feeding, a more natural way of nourishment. As the days passed in complete darkness, my senses recalibrated, and I was left with something far deeper than simply my thoughts. My perception of time dissolved. My mind became attuned to something beyond logic and beyond the limits of sight and sound. At first, there was stillness, then came the visions, and a heightened state of awareness, as if I were tapping into a field of intelligence far greater than my own mind. I could sense energy differently, as though I were feeling with something other than my physical body, and I could see, not with my eyes, but with an inner knowing that defied explanation.

In that darkness, I had a startling realization: sight is not limited to the eyes. Knowing is not limited to logic. Intelligence is not something learned; it is something remembered. The darkroom stripped away the illusion of separation and left me with the undeniable truth that everything is unified and connected and we are far more than we have been led to believe. If I could access this level of intelligence simply by removing external distractions, what else had I been blind to?

You might be wondering whether intelligence can go beyond what is measured in schools.

Well, science is beginning to catch up to what ancient civilizations and mystics have always known.

*"The intuitive mind is a sacred gift, and the rational mind
is a faithful servant."*

-Albert Einstein

Centuries have passed glorifying the servant while suppressing the gift. Now is the time for the next evolution of intelligence by rediscovering the power of that gift.

The Box of Intelligence: Breaking Free from the Conditioning

Picture a bright-eyed child, eager to explore the world, asking endless questions about how things work. Now picture that same child entering school, and suddenly having its intelligence measured, ranked, and boxed into standardized tests, grades, and rigid curricula. The once-boundless curiosity is quickly replaced with an understanding that intelligence is something to be proven, rather than something that naturally unfolds.

You have, no doubt, experienced this conditioning around intelligence. From an early age, students are given labels based on performance, ranging from the "star pupil" to the "troublemaker;" the one who "gets it" to the one who "struggles." The classroom becomes a stage where intelligence is rewarded with gold stars, certificates, and praise, while failure results in embarrassment, shame, or a quiet resignation that perhaps you just aren't smart enough. Yet intelligence is far more than something that is defined by a grade or a test score.

The Science of Conditioned Intelligence

Psychological research supports the idea that fixed intelligence mindsets are ingrained early on. Dr. Carol Dweck, a psychologist at Stanford University, discovered that when children are praised for being "smart" rather than for their effort, they develop a fixed mindset, believing that intelligence is static. In contrast, those who are praised for persistence and problem-solving develop a growth mindset, understanding that intelligence expands with challenge and effort. Her research revealed that children conditioned to see intelligence as fixed tend to avoid challenges, fearing failure will diminish their worth.

The traditional education system, built on standardized testing and rigid curricula, often suppresses divergent thinking, a critical aspect of intelligence. A famous NASA-funded study by Dr. George Land and Dr. Beth Jarman tested 1,600 children on their ability to think creatively and solve problems in unconventional ways. At age five, 98% of children tested as creative geniuses. By the time they reached adulthood, that number had dropped to 2%. The study concluded that formal education systematically erodes creative intelligence, as children become conditioned to prioritize correct answers over exploration and discovery.

Beyond the IQ Model: Rethinking Intelligence

For decades, intelligence was narrowly defined by the IQ test, developed in the early 20th century by Alfred Binet. Even Binet himself cautioned against using his test to determine a person's potential, emphasizing that intelligence is fluid and can change over time. However, society took the IQ test and ran with it, turning intelligence into a competition rather than looking at the full spectrum of potential.

Dr. Howard Gardner's Theory of Multiple Intelligences, introduced in 1983, challenged this outdated model. He proposed that intelligence isn't a single measurable factor, but rather it exists in multiple forms, including linguistic, logical-mathematical, spatial, musical, kinesthetic, interpersonal, intrapersonal, and naturalistic intelligence. This framework explains why someone who struggles with math may excel at music; why an artist's mind works differently from a scientist's; and why emotional intelligence can be just as valuable as technical expertise.

Defying the System: The Innovators Who Redefined Intelligence

Some of the greatest minds in history defied conventional education models:

- **Albert Einstein** was labeled a slow learner in school and later admitted he often learned best through imagination and visualization rather than rote memorization. He famously said, "Imagination is more important than knowledge."

- **Temple Grandin**, a scientist labeled with autism, redefined how we understand both animal behavior and neurodivergent intelligence. Her ability to think in pictures and patterns, rather than words, made her a pioneer in her field.

These pioneers remind you that intelligence cannot be confined to a single metric. It is not something you passively receive through schooling, but rather it's something you activate, expand, and embody in your own unique way.

The Expansion of Intelligence Beyond the Traditional View

We live in a world that reveres **IQ (Intellectual Intelligence),** increasingly values **EQ (Emotional Intelligence)**, and is beginning to recognize **SQ (Spiritual Intelligence)**. What if there is an even greater form of intelligence that integrates, contains, and transcends all previous forms? **Multi-Dimensional Intelligence** is this next evolution, an intelligence that allows you to perceive reality beyond your five senses, beyond linear thinking, and beyond the conditioned limits of the mind.

IQ: The Measured Mind

For over a century, the **IQ (Intelligence Quotient)** has been considered the gold standard for measuring intelligence. It is the foundation upon which modern educational and professional systems were built, defining intelligence as the ability to reason, solve problems, and process information efficiently.

Lewis Terman at Stanford University refined Alfred Binet's' first standardized intelligence test, leading to the creation of the widely used Stanford-Binet Intelligence Scale. These tests rank intelligence using a bell curve, where an average IQ is 100, and scores above 130 indicate high intelligence.

However, while IQ tests measure cognitive abilities such as logical reasoning, memory, and problem-solving, they do not assess creativity, intuition, adaptability, or emotional intelligence, factors that are just as critical to success and fulfillment. Many individuals with a high IQ struggle in areas such as decision-making, relationships, or even basic life skills, proving that intelligence is far more complex than a number on a test.

The Brain as a Filter: What We Are Missing

Understanding IQ also requires an understanding of how the human brain processes information. Neuroscientists suggest that our conscious mind can only process seven plus or minus two pieces of information at a time (Miller's Law). This means that at any given moment, you are filtering out the vast majority of the sensory data around you, selecting only what your brain deems relevant.

This filtering process, known in psychology as **Deletion, Distortion, and Generalization,** is essential for managing the overwhelming influx of stimuli you encounter every second. Without it, you would be paralyzed by the sheer amount of data available to you. While these filters help you to function, they also create blind spots that shape your perception of reality. This could explain why many geniuses and innovators see the world differently; they break free from these cognitive filters and perceive what others overlook.

Let's explore how these filters work in everyday life.

1. Deletion: Filtering Out What We Don't Notice

Deletion occurs when the brain ignores or removes information that it deems unimportant or irrelevant. This happens constantly, because you are being bombarded with millions of bits of sensory input every second—from sights, sounds, smells, and tastes, to conversations, background noise, bodily sensations, and more. It would be overwhelming if you were aware of all of it at once. For example, have you ever lost your phone, only to find it sitting right in front of you? Your brain had deleted its presence from your awareness because it wasn't "important" until that moment.

Perhaps you've experienced walking into a crowded coffee shop and noticing all the loud voices, clinking cups, background music, etc. However, soon after sitting down at a table with your friend, your brain filters out the noise, allowing you to focus on your conversation. Then there is selective hearing. For example, when someone calls your name across a noisy room, and suddenly, everything else fades into the background. Your brain has deleted the surrounding noise until that one piece of information (your name) was flagged as important.

While deletion helps you to function, it can also cause you to miss opportunities, insights, or even solutions that are right in front of you. Think of how you might walk into a room and forget why you went there—your brain 'deletes' the information because it didn't seem important in the moment.

2. Distortion: Changing Information to Fit Your Beliefs

Distortion happens when you alter reality to match your expectations, emotions, or beliefs. This is how memories can become exaggerated or inaccurate, how fears grow larger than life, and how different people can interpret the same event in completely different ways.

For example, if you send a text message to a friend, and they don't reply, instead of assuming they're busy, you might distort the situation and think, *They must be ignoring me*, or *They don't like me anymore!* In reality, they might have been driving at the time or in a meeting.

If you're afraid of public speaking, perhaps it's because you imagine everyone in the audience is judging you harshly, when in fact, most people are distracted or thinking about themselves and their own lives.

Distortion can either limit you or empower you. When you distort experiences negatively, you reinforce fear, anxiety, or limiting beliefs. If you can learn to distort in empowering ways, such as seeing failure as feedback rather than defeat, then you will reshape your perception of what's possible.

3. Generalization: Creating Mental Shortcuts

Generalization happens when the brain creates patterns based on past experiences and applies them broadly to new situations. This is useful for learning, and yet, conversely, it can also create biases and limiting beliefs.

A child who was bitten by a dog might generalize that all dogs are dangerous, even though only that one dog was aggressive. Or someone who fails a test in school may generalize that they are "bad at math" and carry that belief for years, even though one bad test score does not define intelligence.

Another example is stereotyping. People sometimes assume that all members of a certain group think or behave the same way based on one experience or on cultural conditioning.

While generalization helps you learn quickly (e.g., "stoves are hot"), it limits your personal growth when you apply past experiences too rigidly. Breaking free from harmful generalizations allows you to expand your intelligence and see new possibilities.

Beyond IQ: The Genius Mindset

Deletion, Distortion, and Generalization are natural cognitive functions. Your awareness of them can help you to break free from mental conditioning. Imagine what it would be like if you stopped deleting creative possibilities, distorting reality through fear, and generalizing from your past experiences and limiting your future potential.

Multi-Dimensional Intelligence is an intelligence that allows you to move beyond the filters of the mind and into expanded perception.

What separates a genius from someone with a high IQ is the ability to see connections others do not, to think in multiple dimensions, and to approach problems with both logic and creativity.

Throughout history, individuals such as Leonardo da Vinci, Nikola Tesla, and Marie Curie have exhibited a genius mindset because of their ability to blend logic, intuition, and multi-dimensional thinking. They broke through conventional limits of intelligence and engaged in ways of knowing that were not easily measured.

Testing Your Own Mental Processing

Read the following list of numbers, then close your eyes and see how many you can recall.

4, 8, 15, 23, 42, 7, 31, 90, 56

Most people can recall only 5 of the 9 numbers before their memory starts to fade. This demonstrates how your cognitive capacity operates within defined limits that can be expanded through training and neuroplasticity.

Modern research supports this distinction. Studies on divergent thinking, a key component of creativity, show that those who score highly in this area often outperform individuals with a high IQ in real-world problem-solving. Dr. Rex Jung, a neuroscientist studying creativity, found that high intelligence alone does not predict genius-level innovation; rather, it is the ability to connect disparate ideas, to operate with cognitive flexibility, and to access unconventional insights.

This suggests that intelligence should not just be measured; it should be expanded. And this expansion leads directly to Multi-Dimensional Intelligence, the next level of human evolution.

The Limits of IQ

While valuable, IQ has several key limitations:

- It measures only logical and analytical thinking, ignoring intuition, creativity, and adaptability.

- It doesn't predict success or fulfillment, as emotional and social skills often outweigh raw intelligence.

- It assumes intelligence is fixed, whereas research on neurogenesis proves we can rewire and enhance our brain function at any age.

While IQ is a useful metric, it is merely a piece of the intelligence puzzle. True intelligence encompasses much more in terms of emotional depth, creativity, intuition, and even the ability to perceive beyond the physical world.

After all, what good is a sharp mind if it lacks emotional awareness? What value is intellectual brilliance without the ability to connect, empathize, and navigate the complexities of human relationships?

EQ: The Heart's Intelligence

For centuries, humans have debated the role of the heart. Is it merely a biological pump moving blood throughout the body, or is it something far more profound? Many ancient civilizations revered the heart as the seat of the soul and the center of intelligence. In fact, the Egyptians discarded the brain as unimportant while mummifying bodies, but ensured the heart remained intact, believing it to be the core of wisdom and identity. Similarly, in many spiritual traditions, the heart is seen as the bridge between the physical and the energetic, the material and the unseen realms.

The Rise of Emotional Intelligence: Daniel Goleman's Contribution

In 1995, psychologist Daniel Goleman published *Emotional Intelligence: Why It Can Matter More Than IQ*, a book that reshaped how the world understood intelligence. Goleman's research was built on earlier work by psychologists Peter Salovey and John Mayer, who first coined the term Emotional Intelligence (EQ) in 1990.

Goleman identified five key components of EQ:

1. Self-awareness: understanding your emotions and how they affect thoughts and behavior.
2. Self-regulation: managing emotions in healthy ways and adapting to changing circumstances.
3. Motivation: using emotions to pursue goals with energy and persistence.
4. Empathy: recognizing the emotions of others and responding appropriately.
5. Social skills: building relationships, navigating social networks, and inspiring others.

Modern research from the HeartMath Institute expands on the role of the heart in intelligence.

The heart has its own neural network, often called the heart-brain, containing over 40,000 neurons, which allows it to process information independently of the brain. More remarkably, the heart sends more signals to the brain than the brain sends to the heart, influencing emotions, cognition, and even decision-making.

The heart emits an electromagnetic field that extends several feet beyond the body. HeartMath research shows that this field is not just an energy signature but also a carrier of emotional and physiological information. When you experience stress or frustration, your heart rhythms become erratic, disrupting coherence and affecting those around you. But when you cultivate heart coherence, your physiology shifts, leading to improved cognitive function, resilience, and social harmony.

HeartMath studies show that when leaders cultivate a state of coherence, balancing their heart rate variability, they create a ripple effect, positively influencing those in their environment.

Cultivating Heart-Brain Coherence

Try this simple Heart Coherence Exercise:

1. Focus on Your Heart. Place your hand on your chest and bring your awareness to your heart.

2. Breathe Slowly and Deeply. Inhale for 5 seconds, exhale for 5 seconds, maintaining a steady rhythm.

3. Generate a Positive Emotion. Recall a moment of gratitude, love, or joy. Feel it fully in your heart space.

4. Maintain this Feeling. Continue for a few minutes, noticing a sense of calm and clarity arise.

Studies show that practicing this for just 3 minutes a day enhances emotional regulation, reduces stress, and strengthens overall resilience.

This is why great leaders exude an unseen yet powerful presence, making others feel calm, inspired, and engaged.

Limitations of EQ

While EQ is powerful, it has its limitations:

- It focuses primarily on human relationships but doesn't account for higher states of perception and non-local intelligence.

- It relies on subjective interpretations, which can be influenced by cultural and personal biases.

Beyond Emotional Intelligence: Accessing a Higher Intelligence

Moving beyond emotional intelligence, you begin to access a higher level of intelligence, one that connects you not only to each other but to a greater universal field of awareness.

Stephen Covey, best known for his book, *The 7 Habits of Highly Effective People*, emphasized that true intelligence is not limited to cognitive ability (IQ) or even emotional awareness (EQ). He believed that while IQ helps you to think and analyze, and EQ allows you to connect and communicate, neither are fully effective without a strong foundation of inner wisdom; what he called Spiritual Intelligence (SQ).

Covey explained that:

- **IQ (Intellectual Intelligence)** provides knowledge, logic, and reasoning, but intelligence alone is useless if you cannot effectively connect, influence, or collaborate with others.

- **EQ (Emotional Intelligence)** allows you to relate, empathize, and build meaningful relationships, but connection without substance lacks depth.

- **SQ (Spiritual Intelligence)** is the foundation of it all because without a deep sense of meaning, purpose, and alignment with your true self, both IQ and EQ remain incomplete.

Covey saw SQ as the highest form of intelligence, the one that integrates both mind and heart into something greater, allowing individuals to act from a place of authenticity, purpose, and inner clarity. Without it, a person may be intellectually gifted (IQ) and emotionally intelligent (EQ), yet still feel lost, unfulfilled, or disconnected from something deeper.

It is SQ that brings meaning, wisdom, and true fulfillment into the equation.

SQ: The Intelligence of Meaning & Intuition

Spiritual Intelligence (SQ) is what enables you to transcend conditioned thinking, perceive higher truths, and operate from intuition rather than just logic or emotion. Unlike IQ, which measures cognitive ability, and EQ, which governs emotional awareness, SQ allows you to access a higher perspective and one that connects you to purpose, intuition, and the broader intelligence of the universe.

Throughout history, some of the most influential figures, from great philosophers and spiritual leaders to pioneering scientists and innovators, have embodied high SQ. They were able to access insights beyond their immediate environment, tap into deep intuitive knowing, and operate from a sense of profound clarity and purpose.

SQ as a concept first gained prominence in 2000, when author and researcher Danah Zohar published *Spiritual Intelligence: The Ultimate Intelligence*. She argued that SQ is the intelligence that enables you to solve problems of meaning and value, making it essential for living a fulfilled life. Whereas IQ helps you think, and EQ helps you relate, SQ helps you transcend.

Neuroscientists have linked SQ to neurotheology, the study of the brain's role in spiritual experiences. Using MRI scans, researchers have found that meditation and deep contemplation activate the prefrontal cortex and parietal lobes. These regions are associated with higher-order thinking, empathy, and interconnected awareness, and suggest that spiritual practices can enhance your cognitive function, emotional stability, and even your physical well-being.

How You Can Cultivate Spiritual Intelligence

Unlike IQ, which is largely innate, or EQ, which can be developed through self-awareness, SQ requires a deep commitment to introspection and expanded consciousness. It is cultivated through practices such as:

- **Meditation and mindfulness:** quieting the mind to receive insights beyond logic.

- **Journaling and reflection:** asking deep questions about purpose and alignment.

- **Engaging in meaningful service:** finding fulfillment through helping others.

- **Trusting intuition:** learning to recognize and act upon inner guidance.

- **Experiencing altered states of consciousness:** shifting awareness through breathwork, sound healing, or fasting.

The Intuition of Entrepreneurs & Innovators

Some of the greatest breakthroughs in history were the result of deep intuition, sudden insight, and an inner knowing that transcends rational thinking. Many visionary thinkers, scientists, and inventors have described moments of inspiration that seemed to come from beyond their conscious mind, as though they were tapping into a greater field of intelligence.

Michael Faraday, one of the most influential scientists in electromagnetism, had little formal education, yet he intuitively grasped concepts of energy fields and forces that had never been articulated before. His insights, often described as appearing to him in mental images and flashes of understanding, laid the groundwork for our modern understanding of electricity and magnetism.

Barbara McClintock, a pioneering geneticist, revolutionized our understanding of DNA by discovering "jumping genes," a concept dismissed by mainstream science at the time. She credited her ability to "feel" the genome and intuitively sense its behavior as leading to the discovery that would earn her a Nobel Prize decades later.

Buckminster Fuller, the architect and systems theorist, described his most profound ideas as coming from a higher intelligence beyond himself. He often entered deep states of reflection, allowing complex geometric and structural designs, such as the geodesic dome (a spherical or partial spherical shell structure composed of interconnected triangles), to emerge in his mind fully formed. He referred to this process as "tuning into cosmic intelligence."

Goethe, the poet, scientist, and philosopher, believed intuition to be a superior form of perception that allowed individuals to see the underlying patterns of reality. His approach to science, known as Goethean observation, focused on deeply attuning to the essence of living systems rather than reducing them to mechanical parts.

Viktor Schauberger, an Austrian forester and inventor, observed water and nature so intimately that he developed revolutionary designs for energy and fluid dynamics, claiming that he was merely "listening" to nature's language rather than forcing ideas onto it. His work in biomimicry and vortex energy still inspires alternative energy research today.

Throughout history, great minds and leaders have shared stories of experiencing sudden downloads of insight, synchronicities, and serendipitous opportunities when they aligned with higher intelligence rather than relying on only logic. These individuals demonstrated the power of SQ, intelligence beyond intellect and emotion, and a deep attunement to the unseen forces shaping reality.

Accessing Your SQ

Take a moment to reflect on a time in your life when you had a gut feeling or hunch about something that proved to be correct. You were accessing your SQ. Now, try this exercise:

1. **Find a quiet space.** Sit in a relaxed position, close your eyes and take a few deep breaths in and out.

2. **Ask yourself a question.** Choose something meaningful; for example, "What is my next best step?"

3. **Observe the first response that arises.** It might be a thought, a feeling, an image, or even a physical sensation.

4. **Write it down.** Even if it doesn't make sense to you, trust that the insight is valuable.

By practicing this regularly, you strengthen your connection to a deeper intelligence that transcends rational thought.

Limitations of SQ

- Difficult to quantify or measure, making it harder for mainstream adoption.

- Often misunderstood as religious belief, though it is more about inner guidance and expanded awareness.

- While emerging frameworks exist and notable tools have been developed, standardized assessment is still evolving.

Spiritual Intelligence (SQ) is a powerful guiding force that allows you to navigate uncertainty, align with your true path, and access wisdom beyond conventional thinking. It enables you to see intelligence not as something you acquire but as something you remember and awaken within.

Pioneering efforts have been made to bring credibility and structure to the measurement of SQ. Cindy Wigglesworth, author of *SQ21: The Twenty-One Skills of Spiritual Intelligence*, developed one of the most comprehensive assessment tools in the field. Her model outlines four key domains—Self-Awareness, Universal Awareness, Self-Mastery, and Social Mastery with twenty-one measurable skills that reflect spiritual maturity in action. Similarly, Dr. Judi Neal, through her book, *Edgewalkers: People and Organizations That Take Risks, Build Bridges, and Break New Ground*, explores how spiritually intelligent individuals lead with authenticity, purpose, and transformational insight. Her Edgewalker model identifies five archetypes and provides a framework for understanding how spiritual intelligence translates into conscious leadership and societal impact.

These contributions build upon and expand the movement to redefine intelligence itself. Even with established paradigms like IQ and EQ, and now SQ, intelligence can no longer be confined to a single measure. Dr. Howard Gardner's theory of Multiple Intelligences helped to shatter that illusion by demonstrating that human capability spans a wide range of modalities, from linguistic and logical to interpersonal, intrapersonal, and existential. His work opened the door to recognizing and valuing the full spectrum of human potential, including the spiritual dimension.

Howard Gardner and the Theory of Multiple Intelligences

In 1983, Harvard psychologist Dr. Howard Gardner introduced the Theory of Multiple Intelligences (MI) in his book, *Frames of Mind: The Theory of Multiple Intelligences.* His research challenged the traditional notion that intelligence is a singular, measurable entity, such as IQ, and proposed that intelligence is diverse, multi-faceted, and expressed in different ways across individuals.

Gardner identified eight core intelligences, later adding a ninth:

1. **Linguistic Intelligence** *(Word Smart)* – The ability to use language effectively; seen in poets, writers, and great communicators.

2. **Logical-Mathematical Intelligence** *(Number/Reasoning Smart)* – The capacity for logical reasoning, problem-solving, and abstract thinking, commonly associated with scientists and mathematicians.

3. **Spatial Intelligence** *(Picture Smart)* – The ability to visualize and manipulate spatial environments; essential for architects, artists, and designers.

4. **Musical Intelligence** *(Sound Smart)* – Sensitivity to sound, rhythm, tone, and music; demonstrated by musicians and composers.

5. **Bodily-Kinesthetic Intelligence** *(Body Smart)* – The intelligence of movement, coordination, and physical expression; seen in dancers, athletes, and surgeons.

6. **Interpersonal Intelligence** *(People Smart)* – The ability to understand, interact with, and influence others; a key trait of great leaders, teachers, and therapists.

7. **Intrapersonal Intelligence** *(Self Smart)* – Deep self-awareness, emotional insight, and the ability to reflect on one's own inner world; often found in philosophers and spiritual teachers.

8. **Naturalistic Intelligence** *(Nature Smart)* – Sensitivity to the natural world, an intuitive connection with plants, animals, and ecosystems; common among biologists, conservationists, and indigenous wisdom keepers.

9. **Existential Intelligence** (*Big Picture Smart*) – The ability to ponder profound questions about life, the universe, and human existence; often linked to spirituality, philosophy, and theoretical physics.

By recognizing that intelligence is not one-dimensional but a vast spectrum of human potential, Gardner's theory reshaped education, psychology, and leadership.

Expanding the Definition of Intelligence

From IQ (intellectual intelligence) to EQ (emotional intelligence) and SQ (spiritual intelligence), and now, with Gardner's Multiple Intelligences, it becomes clear that intelligence cannot be confined to a single metric or definition. Instead, it is a dynamic, evolving phenomenon and one that extends beyond conventional thinking.

However, is intelligence still evolving?

John Grandy's concept of *DNA Consciousness* suggests that intelligence is not just a neurological function but a fundamental property of life itself. DNA, the blueprint of biological life, operates beyond the material, interacting with quantum forces that shape perception, memory, and even evolution. This challenges the classical view of intelligence as a function of the brain alone.

If DNA possesses its own form of consciousness (able to store, transmit, and evolve information), then human intelligence must be redefined. Instead of being a fixed, measurable quantity, intelligence is an evolving, multi-layered phenomenon that connects us to a greater cosmic intelligence.

Grandy's research indicates that changes in neurological consciousness are directly tied to changes in DNA. This means that when your DNA evolves, so does your intelligence, which suggests that intelligence is not static; it is something that can be activated, expanded, and accelerated.

From this perspective, *Multi-Dimensional Intelligence is about more than simply expanding your intelligence. It's about unlocking the latent capacities within your DNA, reactivating your highest potential, and reconnecting to multi-dimensional awareness.*

You now stand at the precipice of a new paradigm.

The next chapter explores Multi-Dimensional Intelligence, a framework that integrates and expands upon all previous models, unlocking the next frontier of human potential, perception, and evolution.

INTEGRATION KEYS
The Evolution of Intelligence - Beyond IQ, EQ & SQ

- The 21st century demands a new kind of intelligence that moves beyond logic or emotion. Multi-Dimensional Intelligence opens the door to a wider spectrum of perception, allowing consciousness to be experienced as layered, holographic, and non-linear and to activate a deeper architecture of knowing.

- Where IQ measures reasoning, EQ measures empathy, and SQ measures meaning, Multi-Dimensional Intelligence measures awareness of the multi-dimensional self. It accounts for intuition, energy sensitivity, and timeline fluency. These faculties are present but often dormant, waiting to be reclaimed.

- The evolution of intelligence moves inward and outward simultaneously, expanding in spirals like consciousness itself. Every limit you've accepted can be transmuted into a gateway for deeper insight, coherence, and clarity of being.

- Your field, your form, and your frequency are intelligent systems of information, always in communication. As you develop Multi-Dimensional Intelligence, you begin to notice how intelligence is expressed through feeling, knowing, sensing, and subtle forms of awareness beyond cognition.

- Multi-Dimensional Intelligence activates when you begin to track patterns, feedback loops, and energy shifts. It enhances your ability to harmonize your inner world with the outer field of experience, awakening new levels of precision and possibility.

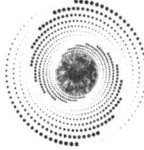

Chapter Two

The Next Evolution: Multi-Dimensional Intelligence and Consciousness

Introduction

Peering Beyond the Illusion

Have you ever woken up with a sudden knowing... an insight that appears from nowhere, yet feels undeniably true? Can you recall a time when you sensed something before it happened, as if reality had whispered its secrets to you? Those moments may seem like coincidences, yet they are glimpses into a much larger field of intelligence that exists beyond the physical world. Consciousness is something you tune into, like a cosmic internet waiting to be accessed.

Beyond the visible world lies a vast, unseen architecture of forces that shape your awareness and guide your thoughts and perceptions. Throughout history, those who dared to question the nature of reality found themselves peering into something mysterious and profound beyond human understanding. Madame Blavatsky and Alice Bailey were among these pioneers, visionaries who suggested that intelligence is not confined to the brain or body but woven into the very fabric of existence itself.

Blavatsky's esoteric teachings spoke of hidden wisdom and a hidden world that transcends time. A vast, interdimensional field of knowledge accessible to those willing to step beyond the conditioning of the physical senses. She introduced the idea that humanity's awareness is obscured by layers of programming that keep you tied to a narrow reality. Alice Bailey expanded on this idea, describing a cosmic hierarchy of intelligence in which human consciousness is only a fragment of a much greater multi-dimensional design.

Increasingly, it appears that the brain may not generate consciousness, so much as decode or receive it, like a radio picking up signals from a greater field.

The ideas set forth about consciousness, from mystics to quantum theorists, challenge the assumption that consciousness is an isolated phenomenon. Instead, it points to consciousness as a vast, non-local field of information that you can tune into, shift through, and expand within to experience different frequencies of reality, much like the keys of a piano. All the notes exist simultaneously, yet the melody you experience depends on which keys are played. In the same way, shifting awareness opens entirely new harmonies of reality.

When you begin to entertain the possibility that your consciousness exists beyond the physical self, everything shifts. Intelligence is no longer something to be measured or standardized. It becomes a dynamic, ever-expanding force that connects you to realms of insight, creativity, and knowing that far exceed conventional ways of thinking.

Multi-Dimensional Intelligence invites you to explore this uncharted terrain. It is an invitation to move beyond intellectual analysis, emotional literacy, or even spiritual understanding, into a realm where intelligence is fluid, intuitive, and cosmic in scale. To embrace the multi-dimensional is to acknowledge that you are an intricate, multi-layered expression of consciousness capable of accessing the unseen forces that shape reality.

Your intelligence has the capacity to perceive beyond the physical to sense subtle energy, and to interact with multi-dimensional layers of existence. The reality you've been taught may only reflect a fraction of the totality available to you.

As you journey through this chapter, you will begin to unravel the essence of consciousness itself. To understand Multi-Dimensional Intelligence is to step onto a path of discovery, one that challenges long-held beliefs and opens the pathway to a radically expanded paradigm of awareness.

KEY QUESTIONS FOR EXPLORATION IN CHAPTER TWO

◊   What if you are a receiver tuning into a greater field of intelligence?

◊   Could your thoughts and identity be echoes of a cosmic intelligence encoded in your DNA?

◊   If consciousness is non-local, what becomes possible when you access more of it?

The Mystery of Consciousness

Consider this scenario... A woman dreams of a red book falling from a shelf. The next day, she walks into a bookstore, and a red book falls onto the floor right in front of her, just like in her dream. Coincidence? Or a glimpse into a greater intelligence at play?

You are aware that you are reading these words, but did you ever ask yourself who or what is doing the reading? And beyond that, what is it within you that knows you are aware? This self-reflective loop lies at the heart of one of the greatest mysteries humanity continues to face: the nature of consciousness.

Some describe the mind as a biological computer, generating thoughts and emotions internally. Yet an emerging view suggests that consciousness does not originate in the brain at all. Instead, the brain may function more like a Wi-Fi router, receiving, transmitting, and interpreting signals from a vast field of intelligence. Just as the internet doesn't live inside your laptop but is accessed through it, your thoughts, emotions, and perceptions may be downloads from a shared, multi-dimensional field of consciousness that exists beyond you.

Despite decades of exploration by scientists, mystics, and philosophers, consciousness remains elusive. Some still attempt to define it solely as a byproduct of brain activity. Yet the increasing evidence suggests otherwise, pointing to consciousness as a foundational element of existence itself.

> "Everything has, or is, consciousness. From the days of the double-slit experiment to the rise of post-materialistic science, it's clear that our thoughts and awareness influence the outcome. Science is now postulating what mystics have long intuited: that consciousness is the basis of all reality. There's a uniting intelligence influencing not just us, but the entire animal kingdom and natural world."
> —John Paul Eagleheart, Shaman & Sacred Site Whisperer

To explore Multi-Dimensional Intelligence, you must be willing to break free from outdated models that reduce awareness to mere neurological processes. Consciousness appears to extend beyond physical form, as suggested by accounts of near-death experiences, remote viewing, and moments of spontaneous, creative insight. These phenomena hint at an intelligence that is not confined, but expansive.

The Brain: A Receiver, Not the Source

For decades, the field of neuroscience has maintained that consciousness arises from complex brain activity. Multi-Dimensional Intelligence invites us to flip this script. It asks you to consider that consciousness is not the end-product of matter, but the primal force behind it; the source code of existence itself.

Consciousness is not a byproduct of the brain. It is the very field from which time, space, and matter arise. It is the architect, not the artifact.

Emerging research in neuroscience based on studying deeply transformative human experiences point to a different model that views the brain not as the originator but as the receiver.

A radio doesn't create the music broadcast from a station; it simply tunes into it. Your brain may function as a biological interface attuning to specific frequencies of awareness. Rather than producing consciousness, it may access and decode it from a much larger, multi-dimensional field of intelligence.

Compelling clues that support this perspective include:

1. **Near-Death Experiences (NDEs):** Thousands of cases report individuals observing their own bodies from above while brain activity is completely absent. This has been reinforced by Dr. Pim van Lommel's NDE Research, which revealed that patients who were clinically dead had later recounted experiences with details that could be independently verified.

Dr. Raymond Moody, a pioneer in the field of NDE research, documented thousands of cases in his book, *Life After Life*, revealing strikingly similar reports from people who had been declared clinically dead. Many describe the following phenomena:

- A sensation of leaving the body and observing doctors working on them from above.

- A life review, where they see events from their past in vivid detail, often from the perspective of others they interacted with.

- Encounters with non-physical beings or deceased loved ones who communicate through thought.

- Returning to the body reluctantly, as if they were given a choice to stay or come back.

If consciousness were solely the product of brain activity, how could people with no recorded neural function report detailed, verifiable accounts of events occurring while they were clinically dead?

The AWARE Study: Verifying Consciousness Beyond Death

Dr. Sam Parnia led the AWARE (AWAreness during REsuscitation) study, a multi-hospital research project designed to investigate out-of-body experiences during cardiac arrest. Remarkably, some patients reported seeing details from above their bodies and recalling specific conversations that were later verified by medical staff.

These cases challenge the materialist view that the brain solely generates consciousness. Instead, they support the idea that awareness can exist independently of the physical body.

2. **Remote Viewing & Out-of-Body Experiences:** Research findings suggest that human consciousness extends beyond the brain and can access information across vast distances.

In the 1970s, the CIA and U.S. military funded Project Stargate, a classified program studying remote viewing: the ability to perceive and describe locations beyond physical reach. Physicists Russell Targ and Hal Puthoff trained participants, including the renowned psychic Ingo Swann, to use non-local awareness to locate targets with remarkable accuracy.

Swann even described Jupiter's ring system before NASA officially discovered it. His insights raised a profound question: If our minds can perceive beyond the limits of the body, are we tapping into an interconnected quantum field?

This aligns with the theory of quantum non-locality, where entangled particles influence each other instantaneously across vast distances, suggesting that consciousness itself may be non-local.

3. **Creative Downloads & Automatic Writing:** Beyond scientific studies, some of history's greatest thinkers, artists, and inventors have described their most inspired works as if it was not generated by their minds but "downloaded" or received from an external or higher intelligence.

- **Mozart** claimed he "heard" entire symphonies fully formed before writing a single note.

- **Paul McCartney** awoke with the melody of "Yesterday" in his head, feeling as though it had been given to him.

- **Jane Roberts**, through automatic writing, downloaded the *Seth Material*, a body of metaphysical knowledge that many believe transcended the ordinary intellect.

If creativity, intuition, and insight do not originate purely from the brain, could they be transmissions from a larger field of intelligence?

When you take this perspective, it shifts everything. Instead of viewing intelligence as trapped within the skull, you begin to see it as a vast, multi-dimensional phenomenon and one that the brain interacts with but does not generate.

If intelligence exists beyond individual awareness, then perhaps the creative process is not about inventing, but about *remembering*, *retrieving*, or *receiving* from a field of intelligence that is always present.

Consciousness Beyond the Individual

Imagine waking up inside a dream and realizing that you can shape it with your thoughts. If reality is consciousness-based, then developing Multi-Dimensional Intelligence is like becoming lucid in the dream of life, learning how to perceive beyond the illusion.

A useful metaphor is that of the ocean and the waves. Imagine each individual consciousness as a wave rising from the ocean. While the wave has its own unique form, it is never separate from the vast body of water beneath it. Similarly, what you experience as "your" consciousness may simply be a localized expression of a much greater, universal intelligence. This aligns with mystical traditions, quantum physics, and the growing understanding that consciousness is fundamental, not incidental.

As Thai journalist and spiritual thinker Suthichai Yoon once described it:

"When you are born, you are like a single drop of water, flying upward, separated from the one giant consciousness. You get older... you descend back down... you die. Then your drop merges again with the ocean. You return home."

This poetic framing echoes the idea that your essence never truly separates from Source, it simply experiences form, then returns to formlessness. Death, then, is not an ending, but a reintegration. Consciousness is not something you have, it is what you are, temporarily shaped and eternally connected.

Groundbreaking Theories on Consciousness

1. Panpsychism: Consciousness is Everywhere

One of the most radical and intriguing theories is panpsychism, which proposes that consciousness is not exclusive to humans or complex life forms; it is a fundamental property of the universe. This means that everything, from the atoms in your body to the vast structures of galaxies, possesses some degree of awareness.

During a visit to Glastonbury's Chalice Well, nestled between the Tor and Chalice Hill, I experienced a profound connection that resonated deeply with the concept of panpsychism. This ancient spring, often referred to as "The Blood Well" due to its iron-rich, reddish waters, has been a site of continuous human reverence for over two millennia. Legend holds that Joseph of Arimathea buried or washed the Holy Grail at this very spot, causing the waters to flow red, symbolizing the blood of Christ. This intertwining of myth and natural phenomenon evokes a sense of living history, as if the land itself holds memories and awareness.

As I wandered through the tranquil gardens surrounding the well, the air seemed to hum with subtle energy, and the vibrant flora appeared to acknowledge my presence. It was as though every element, the stones, the water, the plants; possessed their own form of consciousness, collectively contributing to the sanctity of the place. This palpable sense of interconnected awareness offered a tangible experience of panpsychism, suggesting that consciousness is not confined to humans but is a fundamental aspect of all existence.

Philosopher David Chalmers called consciousness the "hard problem" of science because it cannot be explained through material processes alone. Panpsychism offers an alternative: just as mass and energy are intrinsic to matter, so too might be a primitive form of consciousness. This idea challenges the assumption that awareness emerges only when matter becomes complex enough to form a human brain. Instead, it suggests that the entire cosmos is alive with different levels of intelligence.

If consciousness exists in all things, then our every interaction, whether with people, nature, or even technology, could carry hidden layers of intelligence. If atoms are "aware," this could explain why environments carry energy and why some places can feel magical or oppressive.

2. The Holographic Universe: Consciousness as a Projection

Physicist David Bohm proposed that the universe is holographic in nature, meaning that each part contains the whole. In a hologram, if you cut it into smaller pieces, each piece still contains a complete representation of the original image.

This theory suggests that your consciousness is not isolated within your skull but interconnected across space and time. Experiments in quantum mechanics support this perspective, showing that particles can be instantaneously connected across vast distances. This is the phenomenon known as quantum entanglement. Reality, in this light, may be holographic, meaning that what you experience as individual awareness is simply a localized expression of a much greater, multi-dimensional field of consciousness.

While visiting the ancient city of Petra in Jordan, and walking through the Siq, a narrow gorge that leads to the city, I was struck by the intricate patterns and colors of the sandstone walls. Each layer seemed to tell a story of geological processes spanning millions of years. As I approached the iconic Treasury, I felt a profound connection to the countless travelers who had walked this path before me. It was as though the essence of their experiences had been imprinted into the very fabric of the place.

This sense of interconnectedness reminded me of the holographic principle that each part of the universe contains the whole. Just as every grain of sand in Petra holds the history of the Earth, you may carry the imprint of the entire cosmos within you. Your individual consciousness is an integral facet of a universal, multi-dimensional awareness.

Energetic imprints are real and measurable. In one striking study, a photographer using a form of Kirlian (or aura) imaging, captured two individuals sitting on chairs. After they stood up and left the frame, he photographed the now-empty chairs by using the same specialized lens. What emerged was astonishing: the chairs still retained a visible energy signature of the people who had been sitting there moments earlier. Their presence had left an energetic imprint that lingered in space, invisible to the naked eye, but captured through frequency-sensitive technology. This kind of evidence suggests that your energy continues to interact with your environment even after your physical body and presence has moved on.

If consciousness exists everywhere (as proposed by Panpsychism), and each part of the universe contains the whole (as described by the Holographic Universe theory), then your observation of reality is participatory. This brings us to the powerful concept of the Observer Effect: the idea that the very act of observation influences what is being observed.

3. The Quantum Mind: The Observer Effect

I remember a moment that perfectly illustrates the power of observation shaping reality. It happened during a simple yet profound experience and one that forever shifted my understanding of perception and its role in influencing the world around me.

I was facilitating a firewalking event for a group of corporate leaders. For many, firewalking is a test of mind over matter, a symbolic act that pushes the boundaries of what is believed possible. Before anyone steps onto the burning embers, their minds are often filled with doubt, fear, and logical reasoning that says, *This should burn me.*

On this occasion, something remarkable happened the moment they shifted their focus.

I asked one hesitant participant to stand before the fire and *observe* it, not with fear, but with curiosity. "What if," I said, "your observation is shaping this experience? What if, instead of fire being something that burns, it is simply energy waiting to respond to you?"

At first, he was skeptical, his body tense with resistance. His physiology then softened, as he allowed himself to see the fire differently, and something shifted. His perception changed, and so did his reality. When he finally stepped forward and walked across the glowing embers, he emerged on the other side unscathed and wide-eyed, marveling at how his intent and awareness had transformed his experience.

The fire was the same. The embers still glowed red-hot. But his observation, his belief, and his awareness had shaped the outcome.

This is the essence of the Observer Effect.

The famous double-slit experiment shows that a particle behaves as a wave until it is observed, at which point it "decides" to become either a wave or a particle. In other words, the mere act of observation changes the behavior of matter. While scientists may continue to debate the mechanics, you witness this principle in everyday life. Your thoughts, expectations, and focus are constantly shaping the reality you step into.

When you apply this understanding to your own consciousness, you begin to recognize the realities you are collapsing into form each day. If your focus is fixed on limitation, struggle, or impossibility, then that is the reality you reinforce. But when you shift your perception and when you acknowledge that reality is fluid and responsive to your consciousness, you move from being a passive spectator to becoming an active participant. You are a co-creator of your experience.

This is where Multi-Dimensional Intelligence becomes essential. It offers the ability to move beyond conditioned ways of seeing the world, to observe differently, and in doing so, to influence the subtle, unseen forces that shape your existence. You can learn to see hidden patterns, identify quantum possibilities, and make conscious choices that shift your trajectory.

A single thought, one act of conscious observation, can influence reality at the quantum level. When you begin to understand this, the scope of what you're capable of expands exponentially.

The Science & Wisdom Behind Multi-Dimensional Intelligence

Up to this point, it would appear that consciousness may not be confined to the human brain but instead permeates all of existence (Panpsychism). You've seen how every part of the universe may reflect the whole (The Holographic Universe). And you've discovered that observation itself plays a powerful role in shaping reality (The Observer Effect).

Consciousness is a unified field of intelligence that connects all things. This foundational understanding is what gives rise to Multi-Dimensional Intelligence.

Across cultures and continents, mystics, monks, shamans, and seers have long spoken of this unified force of consciousness that transcends the limits of the physical body.

I once sat with a shaman deep in the Amazon rainforest. As the rhythmic beat of the ceremonial drum echoed through the jungle, he spoke of the web of life — an invisible matrix of consciousness that connects all things. "The trees are not just trees," he told me. "They listen. The river is not just water. It remembers." His words mirrored the essence of panpsychism: awareness is not simply produced by the mind, it is a fundamental quality of all existence.

The more you expand your perception, the more your understanding of intelligence, consciousness, and reality transformed. Consider the following:

- **Tibetan monks** have trained their consciousness to leave their bodies, describing out-of-body states eerily like quantum non-locality where particles exist beyond time and space.

- **Indigenous shamans** speak of entering the "spirit world" to communicate with energies that modern quantum physicists now describe as the zero-point field, an underlying quantum energy matrix.

- **Mystics across traditions** have long described reality as a reflection, like a mirror. In quantum physics, it's understood that particles behave as if they are entangled across vast distances, mirroring each other instantly, suggesting a hidden connection beyond physical space.

Your physical self may be just a projection and a temporary expression of a far more expansive nature that exists beyond the visible in a field of multi-dimensional awareness.

Developing Multi-Dimensional Intelligence means stepping beyond the limits of the five senses and conventional perception and beginning to access deeper layers of consciousness.

Both science and sacred traditions suggest that consciousness is non-local and that it exists beyond the confines of time, space, and the physical body. When consciousness is no longer tethered to the body, it continues to exist, evolve, and expand in ways that defy the linear understanding of life and death.

This opens the doorway to one of the most profound inquiries of all... the continuation of consciousness beyond the physical realm.

Beyond the Body: The Transition of Consciousness

If consciousness is not produced by the brain but exists as a fundamental aspect of reality, then it continues beyond physical death. Consciousness is not extinguished at the end of bodily life; rather it exists beyond the constraints of time and space.

Many spiritual traditions teach that death is not an end, but a passage. The *Tibetan Book of the Dead* describes the *bardo* state as a phase in which consciousness becomes aware but is unanchored from form as it navigates various realms before its next embodiment. Near-death experiences (NDEs) echo this concept. People report a clear separation from the body, a profound sense of clarity, and encounters with dimensions far beyond the physical.

Science is beginning to acknowledge these accounts with greater seriousness. Researchers at the University of Virginia and the Monroe Institute, who have studied out-of-body experiences (OBEs) and NDEs for decades, offer compelling evidence that consciousness may function independently of the physical brain. What is referred to as "death" might simply be a shift in awareness, an unfolding into another dimension of existence, much like quantum superposition, where possibilities coexist until one possibility is observed into form.

The holographic universe theory supports this view, proposing that your physical experience is a projection of a far greater field of consciousness. In this light, death could be seen not as an end but as a stepping out of the holographic projection of your current reality and into a broader, more expansive reality.

Scientists Stuart Hameroff and Roger Penrose propose that consciousness is rooted in quantum coherence within the microtubules of brain cells. According to their theory, the quantum processes that give rise to consciousness do not vanish at death but reintegrate into the larger fabric of the universe. Consciousness continues, transformed and not lost.

Rather than fearing death, you can begin to view it as a natural expansion of perception and an emergence beyond the boundaries of the body. If Multi-Dimensional Intelligence is about accessing higher levels of awareness, then one of the most profound intelligences is the knowing that you are not limited to this body. You are something far greater. You are infinite.

When consciousness is understood as multi-dimensional and existing beyond the physical body or the brain, a new possibility emerges. Intelligence itself may be embedded in the very fabric of your being and even within your DNA.

Beyond the Brain: Intelligence at the Quantum and DNA Level

Neurological consciousness, the intelligence associated with thought, logic, and awareness, is only one layer of a greater multi-dimensional intelligence. Grandy's *DNA Consciousness* theory provides compelling evidence that intelligence extends beyond the brain, existing at the molecular, atomic, and quantum levels.

DNA acts as a bridge between material and immaterial intelligence, between the seen and the unseen. It is embedded with quantum properties that allow it to store, process, and transmit information in ways beyond conventional scientific understanding.

The key to unlocking Multi-Dimensional Intelligence is to shift your un-

The premise of **Multi-Dimensional Intelligence:**

- Intelligence is not limited to the brain; it is encoded in your DNA.
- Consciousness is not a singular experience but a layered, multi-dimensional phenomenon.
- The universe itself may be conscious, with intelligence existing at every level of reality.

derstanding of where intelligence resides from the brain to the quantum fabric of existence itself.

If intelligence operates at a quantum and DNA level, it means that your understanding of what it means to be "aware" or "conscious" is vastly incomplete.

Why Understanding Consciousness Is Crucial for Multi-Dimensional Intelligence

Developing Multi-Dimensional Intelligence requires a shift in how you perceive yourself and reality. When you continue to believe that consciousness is merely an accident of biology, you limit your ability to explore and expand. However, when you embrace consciousness as non-local, multi-dimensional, and fundamental to existence, you open the doors to profound transformation.

- Consciousness is not passive; it is an active force.
- Reality is shaped by perception, and perception can be expanded.
- Multi-dimensional awareness allows access to hidden layers of reality.

Those with high Multi-Dimensional Intelligence can shift perception, influence energy fields, and navigate reality in ways that defy conventional logic. This includes heightened intuition, telepathic resonance, expanded states of awareness, and a deeper connection to the fabric of existence.

You begin to experience this expanded awareness through direct experience. It is not theoretical; it is trainable. You can learn to perceive beyond the ordinary, beyond the five senses, and access a broader spectrum of intelligence that already exists within you.

Layers of Multi-Dimensional Intelligence: A New Way to Perceive Intelligence

To understand Multi-Dimensional Intelligence, it's important to explore its fundamental dimensions, which redefine how intelligence and perception function beyond the traditional models:

1.Quantum Perception- The ability to sense beyond linear time and space, accessing information from parallel timelines, higher dimensions, and the non-local field of consciousness.

2.DNA Resonance-Your DNA functions as a bioenergetic antenna, receiving and transmitting information from external energy fields, unlocking latent potential and shifting vibrational states.

3.Higher Sensory Awareness- Expanding beyond your five senses into intuition, telepathy, remote viewing, and multi-dimensional perception that connects with unseen aspects of reality.

Observing Awareness Itself

To begin expanding your Multi-Dimensional Intelligence, try this simple awareness exercise:

1. **Close your eyes** and bring attention to your thoughts. Observe them as if they were clouds drifting in the sky.

2. **Now shift your awareness** and ask who is noticing these thoughts? Try to sense the space between your thoughts.

3. The moment you become aware of awareness itself, you step into a deeper layer of perception.

This practice can train you to shift into higher states of consciousness. By practicing this, you begin to shift into a new model of intelligence. one that is not limited to the brain but extends into quantum perception, DNA resonance, and multi-dimensional awareness.

4.Energetic Coherence– Aligning your personal and collective frequencies to create harmony, activate higher intelligence, and enhance physical, mental, and spiritual well-being.

Each of these dimensions offers a gateway to unlocking greater awareness, allowing you to navigate reality with an expanded, multi-dimensional intelligence that transcends traditional cognitive and emotional frameworks. These concepts will be explored in greater depth throughout the book.

Only a Fraction of Our Consciousness Is Stationed Here

While you may often identify with your human self, only a small portion of your consciousness is stationed in this identity at any given time. Your physical brain and sensory organs can only process a limited amount of information, thus acting as a filter that keeps you anchored to this dimension.

The findings of many spiritual traditions as well as modern quantum research suggest that your full consciousness extends far beyond what is typically accessed by the mind. If you could expand your awareness beyond these limitations, there is a vast store of knowledge, insights, and perceptions you might tap into.

If you are only accessing a fraction of your consciousness, imagine what could happen when you begin expanding into multi-dimensional awareness. Recognizing that you are only accessing a fraction of your consciousness is the first step. The next is learning how to expand it.

Expanding into Multi-Dimensional Awareness

You stand at the doorway to understanding what it means to be truly conscious. As your Multi-Dimensional Intelligence develops, you will continue to explore the vast, interconnected nature of awareness, intelligence, and existence.

By shifting your perception, you can step into a greater role as a conscious creator, navigating a multi-dimensional reality with clarity, purpose, and expanded intelligence. The more deeply you understand consciousness, the more empowered you become to reimagine what is possible.

As you continue through the journey of this book, we will explore practical methods for accessing and developing Multi-Dimensional Intelligence and unlocking the hidden potential of consciousness. You will begin to navigate your reality in ways never before imagined.

INTEGRATION KEYS

The Next Evolution: Multi-Dimensional Intelligence and Consciousness

- Consciousness is the field in which the brain arises. To live from Multi-Dimensional Intelligence is to recognize that your awareness is not confined to a single body or timeline, but distributed across dimensions, roles, and archetypes.

- Multi-Dimensional Intelligence is the architecture of awareness expressed through your unique energetic system. It draws upon your ability to tune into multiple layers of information, physical, emotional, mental and spiritual, and to hold coherence between them.

- Each identity you carry is alive in your field simultaneously. Multi-Dimensional Intelligence refines your capacity to attune to these dimensions and operate from the level that brings the most clarity, presence, and power to the moment.

- Your experience of reality reflects the state of your inner field. As you deepen your access to Multi-Dimensional Intelligence, perception sharpens and your choices become more aligned with your highest signal.

- Multi-Dimensional Intelligence is to sense beyond thought, to explore the space where knowing arises without logic, and to honor the vast interior technologies that shape your engagement with the seen and unseen worlds.

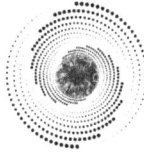

Chapter Three

The Quantum Self: Understanding Your Multi-Layered Identity

Introduction
The Hidden Reality of Who You Truly Are

You wake up in the morning, look in the mirror, and see the familiar reflection staring back at you. What if that image is only a fraction of who you are? What if, beyond that reflection, there exists an entire spectrum of your being that is unseen, yet deeply real?

You are not just a single identity living in a body. You are a multi-layered consciousness spanning dimensions, woven into the very fabric of reality.

Most people have been conditioned to believe that they are only a physical body, that their mind is confined to the brain, and that their consciousness is merely a byproduct of neurons firing. But this is a limiting view. Beyond the visible lies a vast and intricate morphogenetic structure, an energetic template that not only shapes your physical form but also holds the keys to your consciousness, your DNA, and your interdimensional nature. Recognizing this deeper design changes everything. It expands your sense of self beyond biology into the multi-dimensional reality of who you truly are.

The Hidden Map of Our Existence

My journey into the depths of Quantum Morphogenetic Science gave me a profound recognition and activated something I already *knew* at a deeper level. In fact, it felt like unlocking a hidden blueprint of existence, one that explained the multi-dimensional nature of consciousness, the mechanics of energy fields, and the structural dynamics of DNA.

What made this revelation even more astonishing was the realization that my mother, long before I consciously embarked on this path, had already encountered this knowledge. Twenty-five years prior, she had attended a program based on this very information, unknowingly planting the seeds for my future discovery. It was as if life had woven an intricate web, guiding me back to something I had already recognized but my mind had yet to understand.

The teachings were unlike anything I had ever encountered and provided a framework for understanding how consciousness is structured, how realities are formed, and how DNA acts as an interdimensional bridge between fragmented awareness and higher states of existence. More than just theory, this information felt like a transmission and a remembrance of something true and fundamental.

Perhaps that's the nature of all profound knowledge. I believe that when you read a book, watch a movie, or hear something that deeply resonates, it is not introducing something new, but rather awakening something you already know. It is an echo of the wisdom imprinted within, a remembrance surfacing from the depths of consciousness. Sometimes external validation, such as something you can hear, see, or feel, is required to reignite the knowing that has always been there. After all, every thought and every idea exists in the ethers of the cosmos waiting for the right moment to be received and recognized once more.

Quantum Morphogenetic Physics

Quantum Morphogenetic Physics is a pre-diluvian (before the Great Flood) body of knowledge that offers an advanced understanding of energy, multi-dimensional reality, and the morphogenetic fields, which are the underlying template upon which physical matter is structured. It goes beyond traditional quantum physics by explaining how dimensionalization occurs, how consciousness fragments and reintegrates, and how DNA is the key to unlocking our multi-layered identity. It integrates modern quantum principles with the understanding that consciousness, matter, and energy are fundamentally connected through geometric and frequency-based structures. This science reveals:

The 15-Dimensional Time Matrix: a structured framework that maps how consciousness expresses itself across multiple planes of existence.

DNA as a Multi-Dimensional Interface: your genetic structure is not merely biochemical; it is an electromagnetic encoding system that allows for interdimensional access and transmutation.

Scalar Waves and Energy Fields: these invisible structures form the building blocks of reality, influencing everything from thought patterns to physical manifestation.

Merkaba Mechanics: geometric frameworks that explain how energy, consciousness, and physical structures interact across dimensions.

Unlike traditional quantum physics, which often limits observation to the subatomic level, Quantum Morphogenetic Science acknowledges that consciousness itself is an active participant in shaping reality and the force that creates, shifts, and navigates the dimensions.

In this chapter, you'll uncover the layers of your multi-dimensional identity beyond what you see in the mirror and beyond what you've been taught to believe about yourself.

You'll explore how DNA acts as a bridge between dimensions, as well as how consciousness weaves through time and space and the very fabric of reality responds to your awareness. Prepare to enter the 15-dimensional Time Matrix and rediscover the forgotten map of your quantum self.

The deeper you go, the more you'll remember who and what you truly are.

KEY QUESTIONS FOR EXPLORATION IN CHAPTER THREE

◊   What if your current identity is only a fragment of your multi-dimensional self?

◊   Is your DNA a bridge between higher consciousness and physical reality?

◊   How would life change if you accessed more of your quantum self?

Multi-Dimensional Identity & Human Design

A true human is not merely a physical being but an extension of a vast, structured, and intentional cosmos. The body is but one facet of existence, a vessel through which a much greater energetic identity expresses itself. In reality, only a small fraction of your consciousness is stationed within your physical form. The larger portion exists as part of a greater energetic matrix. This expanded identity transcends physical limitations, serving as both architect and sustainer of the body, continuously feeding it life force energy and directing its processes.

Imagine a beautifully crafted marionette on a grand stage. It moves with elegance, responding to invisible strings that guide its every motion. To the audience, the marionette appears to be the performer, yet its movements originate from a puppeteer positioned above, orchestrating the dance with precision.

Your physical body is like an animated, expressive marionette moving through the physical world, while your greater multi-dimensional self is the unseen puppeteer directing and sustaining your experience from a higher plane. The strings connecting the two may seem like limitations, but they serve as conduits, channels of energy and intelligence through which the life force flows. Unlike a traditional puppet, however, your higher self is not separate from you. It is "you" operating beyond the visible spectrum of reality.

Just as the puppeteer remains out of sight yet fully in control, the vast expanse of your consciousness beyond the physical form continuously shapes your experience. The true mastery lies in becoming aware of the strings and realizing that you are the marionette as well as the one holding the strings, with the power to design your reality from a higher state of being.

The Blueprint of Consciousness and Matter

The intricate connection between humanity, matter, and the cosmos is governed by Morphogenetic Fields; intelligent blueprints composed of sound and light that underpin the materialization of both form and consciousness. These fields, operating at both microcosmic and macrocosmic levels, form the very fabric of creation.

Much like an architect's blueprint, which provides a framework for constructing buildings, morphogenetic fields serve as the invisible grids upon which all matter and identity take shape. The universe itself is a vast consciousness field, an interconnected matrix where every possible reality and identity emerges through patterned energy structures. This energetic design creates the foundation for all dimensions and the multi-layered nature of human existence.

If individual consciousness is multi-dimensional, then collective consciousness operates on an even grander scale. Shared thoughts, beliefs, and emotions generate powerful energetic fields that influence and shape the fabric of reality. This is the realm of morphogenetic fields, an area illuminated by the pioneering work of biologist Rupert Sheldrake, whose research offers compelling insights into how patterns of behavior and information are stored, transmitted, and accessed across time and space.

Sheldrake's theory of morphic resonance suggests that when individuals of a species come together, they create a collective morphogenetic field, or a group mind, which influences the behaviors, instincts, and consciousness of the whole. This phenomenon explains how birds in a flock synchronize their movements effortlessly, how schools of fish swim in perfect harmony without a leader, and even how scientific breakthroughs tend to emerge simultaneously in different parts of the world. The field holds the accumulated knowledge and patterns of the past, making it easier for future generations to access and build upon that information.

In human society, you can see morphogenetic fields in action all the time. Cultural trends, belief systems, and innovations are shaped by collective resonance. When an idea gains traction, whether it's a technological advancement, a social movement, or a new health paradigm, it is not solely the product of one individual mind but rather the result of many tuning into a shared frequency of thought. Consider how different scientists discover the same theory independently, or how certain artistic or philosophical movements arise in multiple places at once. This is the morphogenetic field in action; a repository of accumulated thought, energy, and intention shaping reality.

Now, let's take this further. Thoughts themselves create morphogenetic fields. When a certain belief or idea is reinforced by enough individuals, it strengthens the field associated with it, making it more tangible and influential. This is why societal norms, religious doctrines, and collective mindsets persist over generations; they are not just passed down through education and tradition, but are encoded into an energetic framework that holds them in place.

More importantly, this also explains how focused intention and repeated thought patterns bring ideas into materialization. The more people align with a particular vision, whether it be a new way of living, an innovative technology, or a shift in collective consciousness, the stronger the field supporting it becomes. This is the reason that mass meditation has been shown to reduce crime rates, why placebos work beyond logic, and why movements for change gather momentum seemingly from out of nowhere. As individuals attune to the same vibrational thought field, they access and also amplify its effects in reality.

In essence, morphogenetic fields bridge the invisible and the visible, the formless and the formed. Materialization may be an act of will, but it is also an orchestration of collective resonance, where thoughts, intentions, and energy fields align to shape the world as you know it.

Collective Consciousness in Action: Real-World Examples

Abstract ideas about group minds and morphic fields become more tangible when you look at historical events, scientific experiments, and social movements that suggest collective consciousness influencing reality. Below are some examples, from mysterious animal behaviors to global human phenomena, where a collective mind or shared field appears to manifest in the real world.

Scientific and Historical Phenomena of Group Mind

- **Hundredth Monkey Effect:** One famous (and controversial) anecdote of morphic resonance is the *hundredth monkey phenomenon*. In the 1950s, Japanese researchers observed macaque monkeys on isolated islands adopting a new behavior; washing sweet potatoes. As the story goes, once a critical number of monkeys learned the behavior, monkeys on the other islands, with no contact between them, suddenly began washing potatoes. This gave rise to the idea that a new skill or idea can spread through a species via a collective field once a threshold is reached.

- **Group Meditation and the Maharishi Effect:** During the 1990s, researchers associated with Transcendental Meditation (TM) set out to test whether collective focused consciousness could influence societal trends like crime rates. In a well-known experiment in Washington, D.C., in 1993, about 4,000 practitioners were invited to meditate with the intention of reducing violent crime. The research team reported that, during the weeks of the experiment, the city's violent crime rate fell by approximately 23% compared to levels predicted by independent forecasters based on historical crime trends.

If these effects are taken at face value, they imply a form of collective field influence: the meditating group perhaps creates a field of harmony or coherence that radiates out, affecting the behavior of others on an unconscious level. Skeptics argue that these studies suffer from methodological issues or make coincidental correlations. Nevertheless, the idea that an intentional group mind can affect physical reality (in this case, the tangible statistic of crime) is a compelling real-world parallel to ancient peoples' belief in the power of prayer, ritual, or meditation to influence the environment. It suggests that collective positive consciousness could measurably improve social reality, essentially enabling group mind over matter.

- **Global Consciousness Project (Random Number Anomalies)**
  When individual awareness is already multi-dimensional, the combined focus of many minds amplifies that potential exponentially. Together, shared thoughts, beliefs, and emotions form potent energetic fields capable of influencing and shaping the very fabric of reality. Building on this idea, Lynne McTaggart's groundbreaking research, especially in her book *The Power of Eight*, demonstrates how small groups of people focusing their intentions can measurably affect physical systems, healing outcomes, and even global events. Bringing science and spirituality into alignment, her work suggests that group consciousness is more than a concept, it's a tool for transformation.

This perspective is further supported by the Global Consciousness Project (GCP), launched in 1998 at Princeton. Using a network of random number generators (RNGs) around the world, the project has observed measurable deviations from randomness during times of global focus, such as the September 11 attacks, major earthquakes, or worldwide New Year's meditations. These anomalies offer a compelling suggestion: collective consciousness behaves like a field, capable of influencing physical systems. Whether viewed through the lens of morphic resonance or quantum entanglement, the evidence points to a deeper truth: consciousness, especially when unified, leaves an imprint on reality.

Whether or not you remain skeptical, the Global Consciousness Project has popularized the idea that mass consciousness can imprint on and shape physical reality; in line with morphic resonance or "mind over matter" on a collective scale.

- **Mass Psychogenic Illness and Crowd Behavior:** There are historical cases of the collective mind influencing bodies and behavior in more direct ways as well. For example, the Dancing Plague of 1518 in Strasbourg, where hundreds of people inexplicably danced uncontrollably for days; or the Tanganyika laughter epidemic of 1962, where a laughter outbreak spread through schools. Both are instances of what's called mass psychogenic illness. These events demonstrate how emotions or mental states can become contagious and produce real physical effects (dancing, laughter, fainting, etc.) across a group with no physical cause. It's essentially a collective mental phenomenon shaping the reality of those affected. Similarly, crowd psychology in riots or mass panics (like the panic after the 1938 *War of the Worlds* radio broadcast) shows that humans in groups can form a hive mind that overrides individual reasoning. People in crowds sometimes act as if governed by a single consciousness, a behavior first noted by sociologists and psychologists over a century ago. Gustave Le Bon's *The Crowd* (1895) detailed this phenomenon. These examples reinforce the theory that when individual minds sync up with a group, emotion, or idea, the results can be real and forceful, for good or ill.

Expanding Collective Consciousness: How It Relates to You

The influence of collective consciousness has direct implications for your own life. If morphogenetic fields encode and reinforce ideas, behaviors, and knowledge, then you, as an individual, are constantly being shaped by and contributing to these fields. Every thought you hold, every belief you reinforce, and every intention you set feeds into a larger energetic structure. If enough people hold a shared vision, that vision strengthens and becomes more likely to manifest in reality. This means that by consciously choosing where you direct your focus and emotional energy, you can align with and influence the very fields that shape the world around you.

For instance, if you consistently surround yourself with people who reinforce limiting beliefs, you will continue to resonate within that restricted frequency. However, if you engage with higher thought patterns, transformative ideas, and expansive perspectives, you contribute to a field that supports breakthroughs, innovation, and higher awareness, not just for yourself, but for others as well.

Morphogenetic fields act as the blueprints for consciousness and materialization, but they are nested within an even deeper architecture. Beneath human experience and perception lies an underlying structure that governs not only the physical realm, but also the non-physical dimensions of

How can you apply this understanding of Collective Consciousness?

- **Be mindful of your thoughts**. They are not isolated but contribute to the collective.

- **Engage in high-frequency environments**. Join groups, discussions, and communities that uplift and expand your awareness.

- **Leverage the power of collective focus**. Whether through meditation, visualization, or intentional collaboration, amplifying your energy with like-minded individuals strengthens and accelerates the manifestation of new possibilities.

This means you are not just an observer of the world's unfolding patterns; you are a participant in shaping them. The key is to become conscious of your role and make choices that align with the reality you wish to see.

existence. This foundational matrix holds together all layers of reality, weaving consciousness, energy, and form into a unified field of creation.

To understand this, we must explore the dimensional architecture of reality and the way energy and consciousness organize themselves into layered, structured expressions. These dimensions are not separate but interwoven, forming the multi-tiered nature of existence itself. Just as collective thought forms shape human experience, the structure of reality operates through intricate energetic patterns seamlessly woven into the cosmos.

This brings us to the deeper mechanics of existence: how reality itself is constructed, sustained, and influenced by conscious energy fields.

The Structure of Reality

Reality is structured within a dimensional framework in which each dimension represents a distinct organization of energy and consciousness. These dimensions are not separate from one another but are layered aspects of existence, arranged geometrically and built upon crystallized conscious units of sound and light.

A useful analogy is a multi-story skyscraper. Each floor represents a different dimension constructed with unique energetic properties. The materials, namely light and sound, form the foundational elements of these dimensions, just as bricks and steel support a physical structure. Yet, unlike a physical building, dimensions do not exist as rigid layers stacked in a linear fashion but rather are interwoven spectrums of frequency bands that simultaneously coexist and interact.

What Are Dimensions and How Do They Work?

Dimensions are energetic frameworks that define different levels of perception, experience, and consciousness. Each dimension carries a specific frequency of vibration, which represents the condensing of energy into form, and is simultaneously animated by oscillation, which is the expansive pulse of consciousness in motion. These dynamics follow a structured order known as the flash-line sequence: a rapid interplay of vibratory and oscillatory light and sound units that create the illusion of time and space. This sequencing gives rise to the perception of linearity, even though, at a fundamental level, all moments and locations exist simultaneously within the field.

In truth, time and space are not absolute constructs but perceptual experiences dictated by the interaction of our consciousness with frequency fields. **Time does not "pass," but rather, consciousness moves through frames of reality in rapid succession, like a film reel projecting still images so quickly that they appear to flow as a continuous experience.** Each flash of energy is a frame, and what is perceived as movement through time is simply your awareness shifting through these frames in a predetermined sequence.

Similarly, space is not an external, fixed expanse but a holographic projection created by energy organizing itself within morphogenetic fields. The concept of distance only exists because perceived reality is filtered through a three-dimensional framework. However, when consciousness expands beyond this limited perception, it becomes evident that space is flexible, malleable, and interconnected. This explains why certain altered states, such as deep meditation, near-death experiences, or expanded states of awareness, allow people to experience bilocation, instant knowing, or precognition; instances where information or presence transcends the perceived boundaries of time and space.

In essence, dimensions are frequency-based realities with each one serving as the scaffolding for different kinds of experience. Your consciousness navigates these realities not by physically traveling through time or space, but by adjusting its vibrational and oscillation rate. This shift in oscillation changes your perception and opens access to new layers of awareness. This means that what you experience as reality is simply a matter of where your consciousness is tuned at any given moment.

Just as a radio tunes into different frequencies, you do not move physically through time and space. The air around you already holds countless stations, each broadcasting its own program. You don't create the station when you turn the dial, you simply align with the frequency that was already there. In the same way, your reality is determined by where your consciousness is tuned in each moment.

When you understand this principle, you realize that higher-dimensional perception is not about leaving the physical world but about learning to re-tune your awareness. This capacity allows you to transcend limitations, move fluidly between dimensions, and reimagine what is possible beyond the five senses.

Misconceptions About Dimensions

One of the most prevalent misunderstandings in spiritual and metaphysical circles is the notion that humanity is "moving" to the 5th dimension. This phrase is often taken literally, as if the planet itself is relocating to another physical space; however, this is a misinterpretation of how dimensions work. You are not traveling through space to reach a new world; you are shifting your perception to access a broader spectrum of reality that already exists here on Earth.

Since dimensions are not separate locations but frequency fields that overlay one another, the "5D shift" is not a journey in the conventional sense; it is an expansion of awareness. Your consciousness can shift from a limited 3D perspective to a more expansive 5D experience without physically going anywhere.

Another common misconception is that dimensions are isolated realms, completely disconnected from each other. They are interwoven layers of the same fabric, influencing and interacting with one another. Portions of your identity already exist in these higher-dimensional spaces; your consciousness is simply regaining its awareness of them. Dimensional shifts are not about leaving one plane for another, but about merging fragmented aspects of self and integrating a fuller spectrum of consciousness.

Similarly, the term "ascension" is often understood as a hierarchical process, as if one must "climb" from the 3rd dimension to the 4th, then to the 5th, and so on. True ascension is not about moving up a ladder but about harmonizing with one's full multi-dimensional existence. The goal is to recalibrate the self to resonate with a more refined frequency of existence, wherein higher intelligence, coherence, and awareness become the dominant modes of perception.

Dimensionalization: How Reality Unfolds

Dimensions are structured frequencies of consciousness rather than physical locations. Reality organizes itself through a process known as dimensionalization in which energy crystallizes into perceptual experience and forms distinct frequency bands that shape what we recognize as "reality."

This process is not random but follows precise mathematical and geometric principles, much like a fractal unfolding in infinite complexity. Every structure in the universe, from galaxies to subatomic particles, emerges from these energetic blueprints. These morphogenetic fields dictate how energy flows, how consciousness interacts with form, and how time-space configurations are perceived.

Every being, including humans, exists as a multi-dimensional entity, with aspects of their consciousness stationed across multiple dimensions simultaneously. Your multi-dimensional anatomy consists of energetic layers, some of which are already operating in higher dimensions while your physical self remains focused in the third-dimensional experience.

When distortions occur in these energy structures, whether due to trauma, conditioning, or external interference, they manifest as physical, emotional, or mental imbalances. These distortions are the result of repetitive patterns of thought and emotion, which, when reinforced over time, become embedded within the energetic blueprint.

Just as morphogenetic fields act as blueprints for biological and psychological traits, they also encode the frequencies of belief systems, emotional states, and habitual thought patterns. Every repeated emotion or belief strengthens the field associated with it, making it more tangible and eventually translating into physical reality, whether as health, disease, abundance, limitation, or any other experience.

This is the reason healing and personal transformation require more than just external change; they necessitate a shift in frequency alignment. By consciously engaging with thought patterns and emotional states that reflect the reality you wish to create, distortions in the energy field can be recalibrated, allowing the physical form to reorganize itself in alignment with a more coherent blueprint.

- A person who constantly resonates with fear or scarcity feeds into a morphogenetic field of limitation, reinforcing experiences that validate those emotions.

- A person who repeatedly holds thoughts of expansion, vitality, and possibility strengthens the field of well-being, making those states more dominant in their reality.

- Societal beliefs, whether empowering or restrictive, operate the same way. When collective thought reaches a critical threshold, it imprints into the morphogenetic field, making certain experiences more accessible to future generations. This explains why cultural norms, generational traumas, or deeply ingrained societal patterns persist, often without conscious awareness.

This is also why deep states of meditation, energy work, and specific sound and light frequencies can have profound effects on the body and mind. They act as tuning mechanisms, guiding consciousness back into resonance with its original, undistorted state.

Healing as a Return to Coherence

Once you understand the dimensional structure of reality, you can move beyond the illusion of randomness and recognize the intentional architecture behind human experience. Healing is not merely a process of fixing what is broken. Healing is the realignment of consciousness to its natural harmonic state.

When coherence is restored within the morphogenetic blueprint, transformation happens naturally:

- The body regenerates more efficiently, free from the disruptions caused by distorted energy fields.

- Mental clarity increases as higher-dimensional awareness becomes more accessible.

- Intuitive perception strengthens, allowing you to tap into information beyond the limits of the five senses.

This is the natural intelligence of the universe in action. Just as a disharmonious instrument can be re-tuned to play in perfect harmony, human consciousness can be re-tuned to resonate with its higher potential. The key lies in recognizing that thoughts and emotions are active forces shaping reality.

Thus, the mastery of your frequency is the mastery of reality itself.

Beyond 3D: Unlocking Multi-Dimensional Awareness

The true power of human consciousness lies beyond three-dimensional perception. While your physical senses anchor you to the 3D world, your multi-dimensional anatomy extends far beyond it, influencing everything from biological function to cognitive ability, emotional intelligence, and spiritual awareness.

For millennia, this deeper aspect of human design has remained largely dormant, unrecognized and unused. However, by reclaiming awareness of your multi-dimensional nature, you can begin to unlock dormant potential within your DNA, expand your perceptual range, and align with a broader spectrum of reality that is always accessible.

The process of awakening multi-dimensional awareness involves:

- **Activating latent DNA codes** that hold the blueprint for higher intelligence and enhanced abilities.

- **Developing higher sensory perception**, such as intuition, telepathic communication, and the ability to perceive energy beyond the five senses.

- **Recalibrating the spirit body** by restoring balance to the energetic structures that sustain physical, mental, and emotional well-being.

Consciousness operates within an interconnected field of intelligence that spans multiple dimensions. By recognizing that your awareness shifts between these levels, and not through movement but through frequency alignment, you gain the ability to navigate reality with greater clarity, purpose, and sovereignty.

Bridging to the Next Exploration: The Architecture of Reality

Understanding dimensions is about recognizing the energetic framework of existence in which you are already embedded. Just as a radio does not move to find a signal but simply tunes into it, human consciousness must simply attune itself to the frequencies of a greater reality.

This multi-dimensional framework takes shape through precise geometric and energetic patterns that maintain coherence across all layers of existence. Human consciousness is not separate from this design; it plays an integral role within the architecture of reality. To explore this further, let's examine the blueprint that sustains the vast, intelligent design of creation and governs how consciousness integrates into physical form.

The Fetal Integration Process and Consciousness Limitation

At the moment of physical incarnation, consciousness does not enter the body fully formed but undergoes a process of energetic vibrational down-stepping to integrate with biological form. This process, known as fetal integration, serves as the mechanism through which a vast, multi-dimensional identity anchors into a limited, three-dimensional vehicle. However, due to distortions in the DNA template, this integration is incomplete. Upon birth, only a small fraction of your full consciousness remains accessible, leaving you disconnected from the broader spectrum of your multi-dimensional awareness.

Think of a powerful light being dimmed and reducing its intensity until only a fraction of its full radiance is visible. The greater intelligence of your being still exists beyond physical perception, yet your awareness is confined to the narrow bandwidth of the five senses.

Imagine if this restriction could be lifted and your DNA template could be restructured and refined to restore its full potential. This would allow for a radical expansion of consciousness, reactivating your dormant abilities and enabling access to the multi-dimensional identity that remains just beyond perception.

A striking analogy can be found in the film *Lucy*, where a synthetic compound exponentially expands the character's cognitive function, unlocking heightened perception, telekinesis, and control over time. While fictional, the story highlights the dormant capacities within human DNA and the possibility of transcending conventional limitations.

If fully embodied with its original blueprint, human consciousness would naturally operate across multiple dimensions, integrating awareness of at least 12 layers of existence. This is the realm described in esoteric teachings where enlightened beings transcend space-time constraints, interact with reality at will, and manifest experiences instantaneously.

How do you access these higher levels of awareness? And if consciousness is encoded within a larger morphogenetic field, what mechanisms allow individuals to retrieve lost knowledge and activate expanded perception?

A Library of Consciousness: Unlocking Higher Dimensions

Picture an extensive library with 12 floors, each representing a different level of knowledge and awareness. The first floor contains the most basic information readily accessible to all. The higher floors store increasingly advanced wisdom. However, to reach these levels, you must obtain keys, with each key symbolizing a state of expanded consciousness or personal evolution.

This metaphor reflects the multi-dimensional nature of human identity, underscoring the idea that what you currently perceive as self is but a fraction of a much greater reality. Just as new information becomes accessible as you ascend in awareness, your DNA and consciousness act as gateways to higher dimensions, unlocking deeper levels of perception.

Aligned with this view, Chris Hardy's *Infinite Spiral Staircase Theory* (ISST) describes the Self not as a single point of awareness, but as a multi-dimensional being embedded within what Hardy calls a *Syg-Hyperdimension* (Syg-HD). This is a vast, interconnected field of meaning, a kind of hyper-conscious network where each "Self" is both unique and simultaneously part of a collective intelligence. These multiple Selves exist across time and space yet remain unified through a shared semantic or energetic resonance. This framework helps explain experiences like near-death states, telepathy, and moments of profound knowing. Rather than seeing identity as fixed or linear, this model echoes the Multi-Dimensional Intelligence perspective: Self is a dynamic node within an evolving field of consciousness, capable of accessing information and presence far beyond ordinary perception.

By adopting a multi-dimensional model, it becomes clear that Earth and the known universe exist within a harmonic structure, interconnected with realms beyond conventional perception. This interconnected design forms the foundation for multi-dimensional human identity, illustrating that what is called "reality" is merely a projection of deeper vibrational fields.

This energetic framework functions as a harmonic symphony, and human consciousness is inherently woven into its rhythm. The level at which an individual perceives and experiences reality is determined by their alignment with specific frequencies of that symphony. Whether you remain anchored in lower states of perception or expand into higher awareness depends on your ability to attune to these frequencies. This leads to the concept of vibrational down-stepping, the mechanism by which consciousness condenses and manifests within dimensional reality.

Vibrational Down-Stepping: Dimensional Consciousness and Manifestation

Human experience within physical reality is governed by a process known as Vibrational Down-Stepping. All existence originates from pure Source Consciousness, which gradually steps down into distinct energetic frequencies, forming structured layers of space, time, and matter. This process enables consciousness to experience life within a dimensionally reduced and simplified system while maintaining a connection to its original, non-local source.

This structure follows an organized 15-Dimensional Time Matrix in which dimensions are grouped into sets of three, known as Harmonic Universes or Density Levels; each set corresponds to different states of matter and frequency.

For example, consider water, which can exist as ice, liquid, or steam. The molecular composition remains the same, but its form changes based on vibrational movement. Similarly, dimensions represent different states of existence, defined by oscillation rates and energetic density.

Just as the human body is composed of multiple layers of energy structures, so too is the greater cosmos. The ancient Hermetic axiom, *as above, so below* encapsulates this principle, highlighting the understanding that human existence mirrors the universal order.

Within this vibrational framework, DNA functions as the primary receiver and transmitter of encoded intelligence. As physical reality emerges from structured consciousness, human DNA serves as the interface through which that consciousness is received, interpreted, and expressed in form. It is both a biological and energetic conduit, linking the multi-dimensional self to the fabric of reality.

Multi-Dimensional Identity and Human Design

Modern science has only scratched the surface of DNA's true function and its relationship to consciousness, perception, and reality creation. A broader perspective reveals that the original human design extends beyond this reality, originating from higher-dimensional systems that transcend space and time.

Conventional science perceives only a few notes in a grand composition, unaware that the full symphonic arrangement extends into harmonics that it has yet to comprehend. Similarly, human DNA is a multi-dimensional structure, functioning across higher realms of existence, with layers of activation far beyond current understanding.

Consciousness is a frequency-based phenomenon, sometimes expressed as vibration when it condenses into denser fields of experience structured within an interwoven sequence of dimensions. The perception of solidity is merely an interaction between the observer and the energetic frequencies that compose matter. This principle aligns with quantum physics, which suggests that observation influences the materialization of reality.

Returning to the music analogy, human consciousness can be likened to a harmonic arrangement where each instrument represents a distinct frequency band of awareness. The melody of experience arises from the interplay of these frequencies, just as dimensional harmonics shape the scope and quality of human perception.

However, to restore access to full-spectrum consciousness, you must recalibrate the energetic resonance. This involves the reactivation of dormant DNA codes, the restoration of coherence within the morphogenetic field, and the harmonization of fragmented aspects of self.

By recognizing this multi-dimensional framework, you gain access to the full spectrum of human potential. You are not bound by physical form, but are a vast being of consciousness, existing beyond the constraints of space, time, and linear perception.

Multi-Layered You: The 15-Dimensional Framework

To grasp the depth of your layered existence, imagine a Russian nesting doll. At first, you see only the largest, outer figure. This is your physical body, the most visible and tangible layer of you. But when you open it, another figure appears inside. This is your emotional body, shaping how you feel and respond. Within that lies a smaller one, the mental body, holding your thoughts, beliefs, and patterns. And as the unveiling continues, subtler and subtler layers emerge, representing your higher mind, your soul essence, and ultimately your connection to Source.

Just as each doll is distinct yet inseparable from the whole, every layer of your being interlocks to create the complete you. You are a continuum of dimensions nested within each other, from the dense and material to the refined and infinite.

Existence is structured through a 15-dimensional system organized into five harmonic universes, each containing three dimensions. These harmonic universes serve as different bandwidths of consciousness where various aspects of your identity reside:

Harmonic Universe One (HU-1) – Physical Matter Reality

- Dimensions 1, 2, 3: The physical body, emotional body, and mental body.

- This is where most human consciousness resides in waking reality, focused on sensory experience and linear time perception.

- Think of it as the baseline level, where identity is deeply rooted in matter, governed by biological programming, and often unaware of its multi-dimensional existence.

Harmonic Universe Two (HU-2) – Soul Identity

- Dimensions 4, 5, 6: Higher mental faculties, intuition, and deeper soul awareness.

- This is the realm where we begin to reconnect with our soul identity and experience a greater sense of purpose beyond physical existence.

- Often accessed in deep meditation, lucid dreams, or near-death experiences, HU-2 enables telepathic abilities, enhanced intuition, and emotional healing.

- This is the level where karmic imprints and unresolved traumas from HU-1 can be processed and cleared.

Harmonic Universe Three (HU-3) – Over-Soul Consciousness

- Dimensions 7, 8, 9: The domain of higher self-awareness, non-linear perception, and interdimensional travel.

- Consciousness at this level is no longer bound by the restrictions of time and space as experienced in HU-1 and HU-2.

- HU-3 allows for direct connection with the Over-Soul, the larger aspect of identity that oversees multiple incarnational cycles.

- From this state, beings can operate from a collective intelligence and navigate different timelines.

- This is where one begins to access true multi-dimensional memory and recollect experiences from other lifetimes, other dimensions, and even parallel realities.

Harmonic Universe Four (HU-4) – Avatar Identity

- Dimensions 10, 11, 12: Christed or universal consciousness, divine co-creation.

- Here, the individual consciousness expands into an Avatar state, embodying cosmic intelligence and divine will.

- The awareness at this level transcends planetary consciousness and moves into a galactic and universal level of experience.

- This is the realm of self-realized masters, where a full understanding of energy manipulation, creation, and divine principles come into play.

- HU-4 consciousness brings the ability to co-create reality in alignment with Source principles, free of the distortions found in lower realms.

Harmonic Universe Five (HU-5) – Rishi/Ascended Mastery

- Dimensions 13, 14, 15: Pure Source Consciousness, full unity with the cosmos.

- This is the level of complete energetic sovereignty, where consciousness merges back into its original Source state.

- Here, one fully embodies the essence of infinite intelligence, and all aspects of identity dissolve into cosmic unity.

- This level of consciousness is rarely maintained in an incarnate state but is instead the overarching field from which all individual experiences emerge.

Understanding Harmonic Universes

I recall having a lucid dream so vivid that I felt I was in another world, one where I knew things beyond my normal awareness. The symbols I was witnessing in my dream had deep esoteric meaning, and at that moment, I wasn't "dreaming," I was experiencing a higher layer of my own consciousness stationed beyond my waking mind. Could this have been a moment of reconnecting with a level of my identity stationed in Harmonic Universe Two or Three self?

What could happen if you were taught to access these states more intentionally?

Your multi-dimensional consciousness is like the internet, and your waking mind is like a single tab opened on a web browser, focused on a limited scope of information. Yet beyond that tab exists an entire network of knowledge, experiences, and interactions. The more you expand your awareness, the more "tabs" you can access, pulling from different dimensions of reality.

Another way to visualize this is through music. Each harmonic universe represents a different octave in the symphony of existence. Harmonic Universe

One is like the bass notes, the foundation of physical experience; Harmonic Universe Two through to Harmonic Universe Five represent increasingly complex and refined harmonics, allowing for deeper levels of understanding, creativity, and connection with Source.

The expansion of consciousness across harmonic universes is governed by the structured unfolding of nested layers of intelligence. These layers emerge in an organized and coherent way, following universal principles that govern energy, geometry, and frequency. This is where science and complexity theory begin to provide valuable insight, offering frameworks to understand how multi-dimensional systems self-organize and evolve.

The Science Behind Multi-Dimensional Awareness

Consciousness is an intrinsic aspect of the universe itself.

While quantum theories such as Orchestrated Objective Reduction (Orch-OR) suggest that microtubules within neurons act as quantum processors accessing non-local information, you can also look at the work of Stuart Kauffman in the field of emergent complexity.

Kauffman's research suggests that self-organization is a fundamental principle of nature. Life does not rise randomly but follows patterns of emergence where complex structures naturally arise from simpler elements. This mirrors how harmonic universes are not separate realms but interconnected layers of reality that are built upon each other, forming an organized, self-sustaining system of consciousness expansion.

His work also aligns with the concept of morphogenetic fields as blueprints of encoded intelligence that allow for spontaneous organization and adaptation. Just as life evolves, not through random mutations, but through structured self-organization, so too does consciousness evolve through harmonic progression, moving toward greater coherence, intelligence, and awareness.

This means that your consciousness is not limited to one level of reality but is part of a vast, emergent system of intelligence, continuously interacting with higher-dimensional fields of awareness.

What This Means for You Now

Understanding the multi-layered structure of reality has direct implications for how you experience life.

Every moment presents an opportunity to expand awareness and shift your perception beyond the limitations of Harmonic Universe One. Whether through meditation, or focused intention, or simply by recognizing the interconnected nature of reality, you can begin to activate aspects of your higher identity right now.

The principle of emergence, as explored in Kauffman's work, suggests that even small shifts in thought, perception, and energy alignment can lead to exponential transformation. By tuning into higher harmonic frequencies, you are essentially tapping into a larger field of intelligence, much like a fractal unfolding into greater complexity.

This means that:

- Your thoughts and emotions shape and reinforce the energetic fields that structure reality.

- By aligning your consciousness with higher frequency patterns, you strengthen the blueprint for expanded perception, healing, and manifestation.

- Just as self-organization in biology leads to higher complexity and intelligence, self-organization in consciousness allows you to move beyond conditioned limitations and reclaim your sovereign, multi-dimensional nature.

Every step toward multi-dimensional awareness is a step toward sovereignty and toward reclaiming your innate power as a creator. By understanding your place within this vast, structured universe, you can work with the forces of energy and consciousness rather than being unconsciously shaped by them.

This multi-dimensional framework directly ties into your physical structure. While consciousness is non-local, DNA serves as the bridge between your current state of awareness and your limitless potential. It anchors higher frequencies into form, allowing your multi-dimensional self to interface with physical reality through a precise energetic architecture.

Just as a radio antenna picks up unseen frequencies, DNA functions as a receiver and transmitter, allowing you to interface with the quantum field and access the full spectrum of your multi-dimensional self.

By unlocking the hidden codes within DNA, you can activate latent abilities, enhance perception, and align more fully with the harmonic structure of reality itself. This is the next step to understanding how consciousness manifests through biological form and serves as a gateway to reclaiming your full potential as a multi-dimensional being.

INTEGRATION KEYS
The Quantum Self: Understanding Your Multi-Layered Identity

- Your Quantum Self is the awareness that interfaces with possibility, frequency, and form. It recognizes that perception is creative and that what you focus on gains structure and becomes lived reality.

- Each moment contains a field of potential. Through presence, intention, and emotional coherence, you influence how that potential takes shape. This is the art of timeline creation through Multi-Dimensional Intelligence.

- When you operate from the quantum field, you navigate life as a dynamic energy system. The boundaries between thought, feeling, and matter begin to dissolve, revealing the interconnectedness of all experience.

- Multi-Dimensional Intelligence activates your ability to observe without distortion, to shift the lens of perception, and to realign with the version of reality that best supports your evolution. The Quantum Self is already encoded in your field, and Multi-Dimensional Intelligence gives you the tools to live from that expanded state.

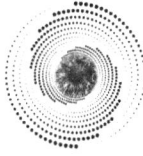

Chapter Four

DNA as an Antenna: Unlocking Your Higher Blueprint

Introduction

Rewriting the Story of You

You may have been taught that your DNA is a fixed biological script, a double helix passed down from your parents, determining everything from your eye color to your predisposition to disease. For most people, DNA has been reduced to a set of inherited traits encoded at birth and sealed by fate.

But this is only part of the story.

DNA is not a static code. It is a living interface and an intelligent system that not only stores information but receives, transmits, and responds to frequencies both from within and beyond your body. It is a blueprint for your biology, your consciousness, your perception, and the reality you experience.

Think of your DNA as an old film strip. When the reel is clean, the story flows clearly. But when the film is scratched or damaged, the image flickers. It jumps. Whole scenes distort. In the same way, when your DNA carries distortions, whether from trauma, toxins, ancestral imprinting, or external interference, those "glitches" show up in your life. They manifest physically as fatigue or illness; emotionally, as fear or instability; mentally, as limiting beliefs; and spiritually, as disconnection or confusion.

Just as a film projector can only display what's encoded in the reel, your outer world reflects the internal frequencies carried by your DNA. When the coding is compromised, so is the quality of your experience.

This is why understanding DNA as an antenna is vital. It is more than a receiver of biological instructions; it is a finely tuned transmitter that picks up information from multi-dimensional fields from your lineage, your environment, your emotions, your beliefs, and even from cosmic sources beyond space and time.

In earlier chapters, you discovered the Phantom DNA Effect, where DNA leaves an energetic imprint even after its physical removal, hinting that DNA is more than matter. It is energy, light, and harmonic patterns. It connects to your family tree and to the universal field of consciousness.

In this chapter, you'll go deeper into this mystery. You'll learn how DNA absorbs and emits biophotons (light), responds to thought and feeling, and holds dormant codes that can be activated for regeneration, transformation, and expanded states of being.

Your genetic past doesn't necessarily mean you are held in a repeating loop. Your DNA is listening... and it's waiting for you to remember how to tune it.

KEY QUESTIONS FOR EXPLORATION IN CHAPTER FOUR

◊ If your DNA is a receiver of frequency, then what signals are shaping your current reality?

◊ What new abilities or awareness might emerge as dormant DNA strands begin to awaken?

◊ How would your life change if you could re-tune your DNA to align with your original, multi-dimensional blueprint?

Breaking the Limits of DNA: The New Science of Self

For too long, DNA has been framed as a static sequence, a molecular instruction manual for coding proteins; a complex but ultimately mechanical system encoding the traits inherited from your ancestors and that make you who you are. New teachings point to a far more expansive role: DNA is not just a biochemical archive, it is a multi-dimensional interface, a quantum antenna, and a bridge to Source consciousness.

DNA as a Liquid Crystal Superconductor

Russian biophysicist Dr. Peter Gariaev and his team in the field of wave genetics discovered that DNA behaves like a liquid crystal and is capable of storing and transmitting information via light and sound. DNA emits coherent biophotons (organized light waves) that act like a laser communication system. These findings suggest that DNA is a physical structure, but much more than that, it is an energetic system that responds to intention and frequency.

His experiments showed that language itself can influence genetic material. When exposed to modulated laser light encoded with linguistic information,

"DNA is a biological internet programmable through frequency, light, and sound." – Dr. Peter Gariaev

DNA would respond. This implies that it can be "reprogrammed" through sound and consciousness.

This understanding echoes the pioneering work of molecular biologist Dr. Mae-Wan Ho, who described the body as a quantum coherent system, a liquid crystalline matrix where light, sound, and structured water orchestrate instantaneous communication between cells. Her research supports the idea that life is not driven by isolated chemical reactions, but by harmonic resonance and quantum entanglement.

These revelations about DNA's responsiveness to light, sound, and intention open the door to an even more expansive understanding of its function not merely as a biochemical code, but as a dynamic interface with the cosmos.

Recent perspectives suggest that DNA operates more like acosmic receiver, finely tuned to access and decode information from multi-dimensional fields of consciousness.

DNA: The Cosmic Receiver

Antenna theory reveals that certain shapes, such as spirals and fractals, are ideal for receiving multiple frequencies. DNA's double helix structure closely resembles the design of fractal antennas used in modern telecommunications. It is perfectly formed to act as a biological receiver.

Dr. Fritz-Albert Popp discovered that DNA emits and absorbs biophotons – flashes of coherent light that serve as a communication system within and beyond the body. Meanwhile, Dr. Glen Rein's research showed that DNA is influenced by emotional states. For example, love and gratitude expanded the DNA helix; fear and stress caused it to contract.

These findings confirm that DNA is far from inert. It is reactive, intelligent, and deeply connected to the energetic field of human consciousness.

Just as DNA may function as a quantum antenna, the mind can be seen as a container of non-physical energy forms including your thoughts, dreams, emotions, and intuition. Olav Drageset in his book, *Consciousness and Cosmos: Proposal for a New Paradigm Based on Physics and Introspection*, proposes that the mind occupies a separate but interconnected space governed by a different kind of energy. If non-physical phenomena can be observed or experienced through a known or as-yet-unknown sense, they must be rooted in some form of energy that is modellable mathematically. This validates the role of DNA as a tuning device, interfacing with both physical and non-physical dimensions.

If DNA functions as a resonant antenna, then it is constantly interacting with an invisible symphony of signals, many of which originate beyond the confines of our known physical reality. In a world saturated with mass programming and environmental interference, this delicate instrument may become tuned to discordant frequencies that distort your perception and behavior. Yet, within you lies the capacity to attune to higher frequencies, those that resonate with your original cosmic intelligence. This recalibration depends on the mechanisms through which information is transmitted and received. Torsion fields (spiraling, subtle currents that transcend time and space) may serve as the conduits for this energetic communication, allowing consciousness to interface with the DNA structure in ways modern science is only beginning to comprehend.

DNA and Torsion Fields: Your Access Point to Higher Dimensions

A torsion field is essentially a vortex of spin, generated by the twisting motion of subatomic particles. Your DNA, in its helical form, generates these torsion fields naturally. These are not bound by the limits of gravity or electromagnetism, they connect your physical body to non-physical layers of consciousness: soul, oversoul, avatar, and beyond.

Think of torsion fields as the "quantum Wi-Fi" that your DNA uses to communicate with higher-dimensional fields of intelligence. When your DNA is activated and coherent, it becomes a high-fidelity transmitter, able to download intuition, spontaneous healing, and multi-dimensional awareness.

So, what exactly are you meant to be tuning into?

When DNA is fully activated and aligned with these torsion fields, it receives scattered signals, and it also reconnects with an original, divine design. This brings us to the Diamond Sun DNA Template, a blueprint of wholeness and multi-dimensional mastery encoded within us all, now waiting to be remembered.

The Diamond Sun DNA Template: Remembering the Original Blueprint

Humanity was originally designed with a 12-strand DNA template, often referred to as the Diamond Sun or Christos Blueprint, known in some esoteric traditions as the Silicate Matrix or 12-Strand Avatar Blueprint. This original genetic design, described in various spiritual and metaphysical teachings, represents the full multi-dimensional capacity of the human being, enabling expanded consciousness, inter-dimensional awareness, and embodiment of higher frequencies.

Each strand is a bridge acting as an interface between dimensions of consciousness and levels of identity. This original template was symbolic, functional, and eternal-life based, allowing for cellular regeneration, interdimensional travel, and the seamless integration of spirit and form.

Today, most of humanity operate with only two to three strands active, and the others lying dormant; not lost, but simply waiting. Waiting for resonance. Waiting for remembrance. This limited activation dims perception, narrows awareness, and veils the innate brilliance encoded within.

But what if more strands began to awaken? And what if your body became a living light temple and an instrument of expanded perception?

With each additional strand activated, new capacities could unfold, such as telepathic connection, instantaneous healing, interspecies communication, quantum-level cognition, and a sense of being both singular and infinite, simultaneously.

Rather than ascending away from the body, restoring the Diamond Sun template is about descending into it more fully and inhabiting your form as a divine, multi-dimensional vessel. You were encoded. And now, the codes are stirring.

As this inner architecture reawakens, a profound realization emerges; you are in the universe and the universe is in you.

The Holographic Universe & DNA as a Hologram

In *The Holographic Universe*, author Michael Talbot presents a mind-bending proposition: that every part of a system contains the whole. Just as a holographic image, when fragmented, reveals the entire image in every piece, so too does your DNA. Every cell, every strand, every subatomic particle holds the blueprint of the totality.

Within each of your cells lies the full pattern of your multi-dimensional being. Even if the image has been distorted through trauma, conditioning, or environmental interference, the full picture still exists within you. Intact. Complete. Waiting to be illuminated.

This is the essence of the holographic model: you are a fractal of the All. Each strand of your DNA is both biological and cosmic. Each step on your awakening path reclaims another piece of the whole, not only restoring your original template but activating the memory that you are and always have been the living universe encoded in form.

Distortions in the Hologram: How Our DNA Reflects a Fragmented Reality

If a holographic plate is scratched or distorted, the projected image will appear fragmented or incomplete. This is an apt metaphor for the state of human consciousness and our DNA today. Many mystical traditions give evidence of this, and the quantum theorists propose that we once had a far greater range of perception and abilities; perhaps even the capacity to access multiple dimensions of reality simultaneously. However, over time, distortions in your DNA, environmental influences, and mass programming have "scratched" the holographic plate, leaving you with an incomplete picture of who you truly are. These distortions are metaphysical, mental, and physical. For example, the toxins you ingest daily through processed foods, contaminated water, polluted air, and chemical-laden products infiltrate your biology, further clouding the clarity of your DNA's signal. It's like trying to see your reflection in a cracked mirror; no matter how closely you look, you're only seeing fragments of your true self. Until the distortions are cleared, the image will remain incomplete, and so will your experience of reality. These environmental assaults dull your frequency, damage your cellular communication, and anchor you to a denser, lower-resolution version of reality.

When the lens of your DNA is clouded by distortion, the reality you experience becomes equally fragmented. You are, in essence, tuning into a lower-resolution version of existence, missing out on the vast spectrum of possibilities that could be available to you. These distortions are etched into you through absorbed energy patterns from your upbringing, culture, and the emotional climate around you and further compounded by physical toxicity such as heavy metals, pesticides, processed foods, electromagnetic pollution, and chemical additives. Together, they script what you believe is possible, dictate what you perceive as real, and quietly erase what you never learn to see. Let's look at the limits of perception in relation to how deeply your awareness

Key implications:

- DNA and the Collective Hologram. If DNA is an antenna that both receives and transmits signals, then distortions in DNA might affect your individual experience and influence the collective reality you perceive. If a large enough percentage of the population holds the same distortions and beliefs based on fear, limitation, and separation, then the collective hologram reflects this back to you as a world filled with division, struggle, and scarcity.

- Reinterpreting "Reality." The Disappearance of the Universe by Gary Renard explores a radical idea; that there is nothing "out there" at all. The world you experience is not an objective, external reality but a projection of the mind shaped by perception. This aligns with quantum mechanics, which suggests that the act of observation determines reality. In other words, the world isn't fixed; it morphs based on how you perceive and engage with it. If true, then your DNA, beliefs, frequency state, and the toxins that alter them, dictate your personal experience as well as the very nature of the holographic projection you call "the world."

is sculpted by the invisible architecture of your upbringing, environment, and belief systems.

Programming, Conditioning, and Perception: The Limits of Our Awareness

Modern science confirms that your perception operates within a remarkably narrow bandwidth. You see only a tiny slice of the electromagnetic spectrum, hear within a limited frequency range, and sense only what your conditioned nervous system has been programmed to detect. While these filters help you navigate a complex world, they also obscure a far greater reality that exists just beyond your usual awareness.

What you experience as "real" is not the full picture; it's a filtered projection shaped by cultural conditioning, societal programming, and the beliefs you've inherited or adopted. Whether through religious dogma, educational systems, or scientific materialism, you're often taught to dismiss anything that can't be measured or neatly explained. These limitations shape your thinking and reality.

Your DNA, functioning as a holographic receiver, is central to this process. When it's dormant, distorted, or misaligned, it restricts your access to higher frequencies of perception. As a result, you may find yourself locked into a reality defined by fear, separation, and limitation. As you begin to repair and reactivate your DNA template, your perceptual bandwidth expands. You start to sense more, feel more, know more, because you've finally tuned in to what was always there, just beyond the veil.

In this new understanding of DNA, you enter the realm of Multi-Dimensional Intelligence, your capacity to perceive and operate across multiple layers of consciousness and frequency, and a model that sees consciousness as a dynamic field of frequencies. DNA, within this model, is an intelligent, responsive antenna attuned to both inner and outer realities.

To view DNA only through the lens of biology is to miss its quantum function. Yes, it codes proteins, but it also codes perception. It shapes your experience by interacting with unseen energetic realms.

Tuning Into the Cosmic Symphony

If you are the radio receiver, immersed in a field of infinite frequencies, some of those frequencies will be distorted by static, while others will be transmitting pure insight, wisdom, and higher intelligence. The frequency you align with determines the quality of your reality. Your DNA acts as the tuning mechanism; the dial that selects which signals you receive and respond to.

Your consciousness is like a television screen, and your DNA functions as the remote control. If fixed on one channel, especially a program filled with noise or limitation, it can feel as though that's all reality has to offer. But when you change the channel, entirely new streams of information, perception, and experience open.

As you begin to awaken dormant DNA sequences, your internal signal sharpens. You start to perceive more than just the surface of life. What once was regarded as "junk" DNA has revealed itself to be a living interface designed to connect you with realms and realities beyond the physical dimension.

This is the invitation of quantum biology: to recognize that your DNA is a blueprint for the body and that it's your access point to the Multi-Dimensional Matrix of existence.

Accessing the Multi-Dimensional Matrix through DNA

While mainstream science still holds that DNA is mostly "junk," with over 98% of its sequences not coding for proteins, this so-called junk is the key to your multi-dimensional nature. Quantum biology proposes that DNA's unused sequences might act as an interface between the physical and the energetic realms, acting as a receiver for information beyond the standard perception of time and space.

Many traditions have long spoken of humanity's potential to access higher states of being. From the Vedic concept of Akashic records to the Hermetic principle of *"as above, so below,"* the idea that you are embedded within a grander cosmic structure is not new. If DNA is a quantum receiver, then it follows that it is attuned to frequencies beyond the three-dimensional reality you typically engage with. The game realm in which you reside, or the simulation, as some quantum theorists propose, is influenced by the state of your DNA.

Your DNA is like the console's access key in an expansive open-world video game. The more strands you activate, the more levels, powers, and hidden realms you unlock. If your console is glitching or running outdated software (from toxins, stress, or programming), you're stuck in the tutorial level never realizing there's an entire universe waiting just beyond the veil.

Experiences of altered states of consciousness, near-death experiences, and spontaneous healing often involve shifts in the way DNA is operating. There is growing speculation that activating dormant DNA sequences may allow humanity to transcend the limitations of physical reality, reconfiguring the boundaries of human potential. The DNA of a spiritually activated individual may resonate at a frequency that harmonizes with the greater field of intelligence, making them more receptive to intuition, synchronicity, and instantaneous manifestation.

From Biochemical Script to Cosmic Symphony

When seen through this multi-dimensional lens, DNA is no longer a fixed code from the past. It becomes a living instrument, tuning into frequencies that shape your present and create your future.

- It is your **personal holographic projector**. The quality of its light determines the clarity of your life.

- It is your **sacred technology**. The bridge between matter and spirit.

- It is the **forgotten language of the stars** and it's speaking again.

The question is: Are you ready to remember what it's saying?

Practical Applications: Unlocking Your Higher DNA Potential

If DNA is truly an antenna capable of tuning into higher states of consciousness, how can its function be optimized? The key lies in frequency, coherence, and intentional resonance. Here are some methods for aligning your DNA with its highest potential:

- **Breathwork & Pranic Activation** – Certain breathing techniques, such as holotropic breathing and pranayama, influence the electromagnetic charge of the body, altering DNA's receptivity to higher states of awareness.

- **Sound and Frequency Healing** – DNA responds to vibration. Practices such as toning, binaural beats, solfeggio frequencies, and tuning forks can activate and align DNA with higher states of resonance.

- **Light and Sun Gazing** – As DNA emits and absorbs light. Exposure to natural sunlight and specific light frequencies can enhance its function and upgrade its informational capacity.

- **Meditation & Quantum Visualization** – Directing focused intention toward DNA can shift its structure. Visualizing DNA as a luminous, spiral antenna receiving high-frequency light codes can aid in its activation.

- **Nourishment and Detoxification** – Processed foods and environmental toxins distort the body's electromagnetic balance. Purifying the physical vessel supports DNA's optimal function as a receiver of higher intelligence.

Repairing the DNA Hologram and Realigning with Your True Blueprint

If distortions in DNA affect the holographic projection of reality, then healing and reactivating DNA can restore a clearer experience of your multi-dimensional self. This is the premise behind DNA activation, energy work, and consciousness-expansion practices: to awaken the deeper codes of who you are and bring coherence back to the energetic structures that shape your life.

One of the foundational methods for restoring the integrity of your DNA is through altering perception and expanding awareness. The Multi-Dimensional Intelligence model suggests that when you move beyond the limited filters of the five senses and linear thinking, you re-tune your DNA to receive broader frequencies of consciousness. This is "thinking differently," and it's about collapsing the old programs that tell you what's possible. As *The Disappearance of the Universe* highlights, "nothing is out there, only within." Reprogramming DNA begins with perception. When the mind shifts, so too does the signal your DNA receives and broadcasts.

Cymatics, a science that studies how sound can visibly reorganize matter into coherent geometric patterns, offers a glimpse of what's possible when the right frequencies interact with your inner structure. With the correct frequency input, DNA can begin to re-align with its original holographic blueprint.

Fasting, pranic activation, and conscious detoxification also play a powerful role in restoring DNA functionality. In my own experience of transitioning to Source Feeding (a lifestyle of nourishment without physical food, also known as Pranic Living or Breatharianism), I noticed that fasting and detox brought clarity to my mind and appeared to unlock new levels of perception. Since DNA operates within an electromagnetic and biochemical environment, purifying the body supports its energetic upgrade. Practices like dry fasting, breathwork, and transitioning to pranic nourishment shift the body's internal resonance, improving the flow of life-force energy and allowing DNA to transmit and receive higher levels of information. These states of internal clarity support health as well as awakening a deeper alignment with Source.

Emerging research suggests that this transformation is not only happening at the level of DNA, but also within the mitochondria, the cell's energy producers. Long thought of as simple metabolic engines, mitochondria are now being re-envisioned as highly sensitive transducers, tuned to light, sound, and frequency. They convert coherent environmental signals into biochemical and bioelectric vitality. When exposed to high-frequency breath, structured water, or states of deep stillness, their resonance increases. But when burdened by deuterium (a heavier isotope of hydrogen that can slow cellular energy production and disrupt biological processes), toxins, or emotional incoherence, their function begins to collapse. This has profound implications. Your perception, energy, and even your cellular communication are affected by what you consume and by what you emit. The mitochondriac view is radical but resonant and suggests that they may be the hidden bridge between consciousness and cellular light.

Finally, perhaps one of the most overlooked yet profound influences on DNA is emotional and mental coherence. Research by Dr. Glen Rein demonstrated that DNA responds directly to human emotion: elevated states such as love, gratitude, and joy cause the DNA helix to relax, expand, and become more receptive; whereas fear and stress cause it to tighten and lose coherence. Your emotional state becomes the frequency field that DNA attunes to. When emotional balance is restored and inner harmony cultivated, you literally recalibrate your biology to resonate with wholeness.

Expanding the Frequency Band of Perception

Multi-Dimensional Intelligence offers a radical shift in understanding perception, potential, and the role of DNA. Rather than accepting the narrow frequency band of experience called "normal," it opens the door to an entire spectrum of realities accessible through frequency alignment.

Your DNA has the potential to tune into vastly different versions of reality. As you refine your awareness and clear the distortions that obscure your inner antenna, you begin to access heightened intuition, non-local awareness, and a deeper connection to the intelligence of life itself.

INTEGRATION KEYS
DNA as an Antenna Unlocking Your Higher Blueprint

- Your DNA is more than biology; it is a multi-dimensional interface encoded with memory, instruction, and resonance. Every strand holds not only physical potential, but also energetic blueprints for expanded perception and higher states of awareness.

- DNA functions as a transmitter and receiver, tuned by thought, environment, and intention. Through sound, frequency, and light, your DNA interacts with the morphogenetic field to access new levels of consciousness.

- Activating your DNA involves clearing distortions, reclaiming original templates, and attuning to the geometry of your own higher blueprint. As your DNA aligns with higher harmonics, dormant abilities begin to come online, clarity sharpens, intuition heightens, and the body becomes more radiant.

- Multi-Dimensional Intelligence opens the gateway to understanding DNA as a living archive of your multi-dimensional self, responding not only to what you ingest or think, but to the frequencies you embody and the futures you claim.

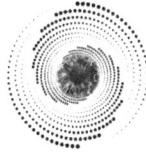

Chapter Five

Higher Sensory Perception: Accessing the Unseen

Introduction
The Hidden Layers of Perception

Since the dawn of civilization, there has been a fascination with those who see beyond the visible world; the ancient lineage of mystics, seers, oracles, and shamans who accessed the subtle layers of reality. Their insights and visions, woven into the mythologies of every culture, speak of something deeper... something dormant yet strangely familiar.

Even in an age saturated with logic and technology, the allure of higher perception persists. This is a recognition that reality is far more layered than what the five physical senses reveal. Deep within, you know that you are not confined to a 3D interface. You've likely had glimpses of higher awareness through dreams of something that later came to pass, an intuitive nudge that proved accurate, or a felt connection with a person or place that defied logic.

These experiences are activations... moments when dormant capacities within your consciousness are switched on or brought into sharper focus, allowing you to perceive and interact with reality in an expanded way.

Higher Sensory Perception (HSP) extends beyond the known senses as intuition, telepathy, energy awareness, and multi-dimensional vision. These faculties are part of your original design. You are wired for them.

Many civilizations knew this. Egyptian priestesses could read energy fields. Mayan shamans navigated dream realms. The Oracle of Delphi received transmissions that influenced empires. And moreover, these technologies of consciousness were universally accepted.

Quantum physics and consciousness studies affirm what mystics have long understood: perception is not created in the brain; it is received through it. Dr. Mohsen Paul Sarfarazi, president of the Institute of Spiritual Science, confirms this view: "the brain is not the generator of consciousness, but a receiver-transmitter interface between your local awareness and the non-local field of intelligent energy."

Your consciousness is the true source of perception and is not bound by space or time. It is a coherent, crystalline energy that flows in from Source, the zero-point field of infinite frequency. In this view, perception is less about gathering sensory data from the outside, and more about tuning inward to receive transmissions from a field of unified intelligence.

How can you tell the difference between imagination and true higher perception? John Paul Eagleheart, a practicing shaman and theatre director, offers a subtle but powerful distinction: "Imagination feels like energy flowing out, both constructive and creative. But higher perception is energy flowing in, an influx, a transmission." He notes that downloads of information are often difficult to retain in their entirety because they are not generated by the egoic mind; they flow through you as frequency.

This distinction helps to explain the concept of hypercommunication, a form of instantaneous, non-local information transfer between your consciousness and a greater field of intelligence. In this view, what is often called intuition or gut feeling is the language of the soul, transmitting insight across dimensions beyond the constraints of time and space.

In a world increasingly shaped by artificial intelligence and saturated by media simulations, reclaiming your higher senses is more than a path to personal awakening; it is a form of sovereignty. Without this inner technology, you risk becoming passive and disempowered by a reality engineered by external inputs. With it, you reclaim your place as an active, multi-dimensional being capable of shaping and steering timelines. A *timeline* can be thought of as a particular path or version of reality that unfolds from your current choices, thoughts, and frequency. At any moment, countless possible timelines exist, some closer to your present trajectory, others radically different and each leading to a distinct set of experiences and outcomes. Higher Sensory Perception is your invitation to lift the veil, to re-sensitize your inner instruments, and to re-enter the conversation between your soul and the cosmos. This is about remembering what you already are.

KEY QUESTIONS FOR EXPLORATION IN CHAPTER FIVE

◊ Are intuitive insights and dreams signals from a deeper, multi-dimensional self?

◊ What subtle senses have you been taught to ignore or doubt?

◊ What shifts when you begin to perceive through frequency?

The Science of Higher Sensory Perception

Perception is not confined to the five senses. In fact, emerging research in both quantum physics and neuroscience suggests that human consciousness is non-local and capable of accessing information beyond the constraints of space and time. As well as observing reality in the present moment, you are participating in a playback of an experience that was registered long before your conscious mind became aware of it.

One of the most fascinating contributions to this understanding comes from neuroscientist Benjamin Libet. In a series of groundbreaking experiments in the 1980s, Libet discovered that the brain initiates decisions before you consciously know you're making them. He recorded electrical activity in the brain up to seven seconds before participants reported making a voluntary choice. This is known as your readiness potential. More recent studies have extended this pre-conscious processing window to as much as 15 seconds. In other words, **the "now" you're experiencing right now actually registered at the unconscious level at least 15 seconds ago**. What you think of as the present moment is, in truth, a delayed construct... a kind of perceptual echo. In fact, your conscious awareness is the last to arrive at the scene.

This insight profoundly shifts how you relate to time, choice, and perception. It reveals that your deeper consciousness, the part of you that operates beyond language and logic, is already interfacing with a wider field of information before anything appears on your conscious radar.

The work of Dr. Dean Radin, Chief Scientist at the Institute of Noetic Sciences, supports this idea. In his presentiment experiments, participants were hooked up to monitors measuring physiological responses like heart rate, skin conductance, and brain activity. Randomly, and without warning, emotionally charged or neutral images would flash on a screen. Time and again, the body reacted before the image appeared, often several seconds earlier. The data showed that the nervous system could anticipate and prepare for an event before it entered conscious awareness.

This suggests that your body, and by extension, your consciousness, is tuning into a field of information that transcends linear time. You are not waiting for reality to arrive; you are already in dialogue with it.

These findings support a growing body of evidence pointing to what mystics, shamans, and initiates have long known: that perception is multi-dimensional. When you begin to trust the signals that arise before the logical mind catches up, you are no longer limited to reactive awareness. You step into proactive perception, navigating reality from a deeper, more expansive state of consciousness.

Together, Libet's and Radin's research implies that consciousness is an active participant and one that is intimately connected to the fabric of time, space, and reality itself.

The Compass of Discernment in a World of Illusion

As you begin to unlock Higher Sensory Perception, discernment becomes essential. In a world overflowing with information but starving for truth, your ability to feel the resonance of what's real becomes your most powerful compass.

This goes beyond dealing with misinformation. After all, you are navigating a matrix of memory manipulation, timeline distortions, and programmed perception. In texts encoded in spiritual traditions across time, there are veiled references to amnesia fields, memory inserts, and false narratives that were seeded into the collective psyche to keep humanity disconnected from its Source.

Take, for example, the Gnostic texts found in the Nag Hammadi Library, which speak of archontic forces; non-organic entities that fabricate illusionary realities to keep souls asleep. Or the Sumerian tablets, which describe the Anunnaki gods as "those who from heaven came," and not as divine beings, but as genetic manipulators who tampered with human DNA and implanted servitude codes under the guise of godhood. Even the Hindu Vedas warn of "maya," the great illusion that overlays reality and distracts the soul from its original knowing.

These are encoded memories, fragments of truth scattered like breadcrumbs for those with the eyes to see and the heart to feel.

Fast forward to the modern age, and the concept of memory inserts becomes eerily familiar. Many people report past-life regressions or spontaneous recall of experiences that feel overwritten, as if they were watching a memory that wasn't quite theirs. Others describe sudden "downloads" that seem out of sync with their internal truth, often followed by confusion or emotional dissonance. These are often signs of energetic foreign interference, implanted scripts designed to keep your perception contained in terms of what you see, hear and feel.

Amnesia fields are another layer of control. These are artificially imposed energetic grids that dull the natural sensitivity of your multi-dimensional awareness. Think of them like psychic static: invisible frequencies that disrupt your inner signal, cloud your memory of who you truly are, and block access to your soul's continuum. Many aware individuals speak of passing through veils of forgetting when incarnating on Earth; like waking up in a body without a map, with only faint echoes of a larger mission.

Consider the compelling research by Dr. Ian Stevenson, who documented thousands of cases where children, often under the age of seven, spontaneously recalled vivid memories of past lives, including how they died and the names of family members. Many of these details were verified through historical investigation, suggesting that memory is not strictly housed in the brain but exists across lifetimes as part of the soul's continuum. These recollections often fade as children grow, hinting at the influence of cultural conditioning or energetic interference and what could be seen as amnesia fields deliberately damping down access to multi-incarnational awareness.

Popular culture hints at deeper manipulation though memory insertion and memory wipes. The film *Dark City* portrayed a race of alien beings who reprogrammed the memories of humans every night, reshaping identities and experiences to control perception. In *Westworld*, artificial beings begin to recall previous timelines, breaking free of their scripted realities. These are not just sci-fi fantasies, they are metaphors for the human condition and living under the influence of a veiled system of reality control.

Discernment, then, is about energetic sovereignty.

It is the felt sense that arises when something doesn't align and goes beyond logic. It's the inner skill of bypassing appearance and asking:

- **"Does this empower or disempower me?"**
- **"Does this create dependency or support sovereignty?"**
- **"Does this resonate with my inner truth, or am I outsourcing my knowing to someone else's narrative?"**

Without discernment, you may fling open the doors of perception only to be flooded with distortion disguised as light. With discernment, you become a master navigator of the unseen, decoding reality through frequency and inner knowing.

In a world of shifting timelines and synthetic scripts, your clarity is your shield. Your resonance is your truth. Your discernment is your liberation.

Challenges arise when the very tools designed to augment your perception, such as virtual reality, neural implants, brain–computer interfaces, and sensory-enhancing devices, begin to replace it, replicating your once-sacred and sovereign consciousness with circuitry and code. The world is now crossing a threshold where artificial intelligence and transhumanism (the movement to enhance or alter human capabilities through advanced technology), are influencing your outer world and redefining what it means to be human.

The Impact of Artificial Intelligence & Transhumanism on Higher Sensory Abilities

With the rise of artificial intelligence (AI) and transhumanism, the very nature of human consciousness is at a crossroads. While AI promises enhanced intelligence and data processing, it lacks the organic, multi-dimensional intelligence that defines human consciousness. The push toward brain-machine interfaces, neural implants, and AI-driven perception augmentation raises an important question: Will artificial enhancements expand your higher senses or sever the natural connection to them?

The human bio-energetic structure is designed to function as a natural antenna to the higher-dimensional realms. The concern is that artificial implants and AI-driven augmentation may override this organic interface, limiting the ability to access higher consciousness states. Instead of evolving naturally through DNA activation and frequency alignment, the risk is that humanity may become dependent on external technology rather than its innate multi-dimensional faculties.

This is a critical moment in human evolution: Either you reclaim higher sensory perception through conscious expansion, or risk outsourcing your abilities to artificial systems that may ultimately control perception rather than liberate it.

Perception Hijack: The War on Inner Knowing

From birth, humanity is trained to trust external authority over inner knowing. The education system, the media, and even spiritual movements often perpetuate programming that dismisses intuition as imagination and reduces consciousness to the process of chemical reactions.

Now, add digital noise, such as EMF radiation, dopamine-driven content, and hypnotic news cycles, and you have a perfect storm - the hijacking of perception.

These distortions act like static on a radio. They cloud the signal of your higher senses, making it harder to trust what you feel, hear, or see with your inner vision.

The antidote? Energetic hygiene and conscious detox. Time in nature. Deep silence. Sunlight. Clean water. Frequency healing. These are now the necessities in the age of distraction.

How Collective Human Consciousness Affects Your Ability to Tap into Your Higher Senses

The morphic field suggests that human consciousness operates as a collective. When enough individuals awaken to higher sensory perception, it creates a resonant frequency field that makes it easier for others to activate the same abilities.

Throughout history, mystics, yogis, and wisdom keepers have served as anchors for higher states of consciousness, holding a frequency that others could attune to. Today, as more individuals reactivate their multi-dimensional awareness, the collective shift accelerates, allowing for a rapid expansion of human perception beyond 3D limitations.

Conversely, mass programming, fear-based narratives, and collective trauma can lower the resonance of the field, making it more difficult for individuals to access higher sensory abilities. The more humanity is immersed in low-frequency states (such as fear, division, or dependence on external control systems), the harder it becomes to tap into the vast range of multi-dimensional perception that is our birthright.

Thus, personal awakening may appear to be an individual journey, and yet it is a contribution to the collective evolution of consciousness. Every person who reclaims their higher sensory perception helps to anchor a new reality... one in which humanity remembers its true nature as a multi-dimensional species.

The Quantum Brain: You're Already Wired for the Unseen

Your brain is a tuning device designed to access the subtle signals of the universe. Neurosurgeon Francisco Di Biase, building on the work of quantum pioneers like David Bohm and Karl Pribram, proposes that the brain functions like a holographic receiver. Rather than generating consciousness, it interfaces with a vast field of intelligence that exists beyond time and space.

He calls this the holoinformational field, a kind of cosmic internet of meaning, energy, and intelligence. In this model, memory is not simply stored in neural tissue; instead, the brain acts as a receiver and interpreter, translating signals drawn from this greater field.

This is vividly illustrated by Dr. Jill Bolte Taylor, a neuroanatomist who experienced a massive stroke that shut down the left hemisphere of her brain, responsible for logic, language, and linear identity. During this time, she encountered a profound state of expanded awareness: timeless, wordless, and euphoric. She could still feel her body, but her sense of separateness dissolved. In her words, she "stepped into the consciousness of the right hemisphere," experiencing herself as energy, connected to all that is. Her experience revealed something profound: consciousness doesn't disappear when brain function falters, it reveals its true, non-local nature.

Seen this way, the brain does not originate consciousness. It acts as a lens, filter, or translator, modulating the boundless signal of Source, already accessed at the cellular level through DNA, into a localized experience of "self." It is less a generator than a multi-dimensional radio dial, tuning what DNA is already transmitting and receiving.

You've likely felt this yourself. At moments when you just *knew* something was about to happen. Or when you walked into a room and sensed the energy shift before a word was spoken. Or in dreams that felt like memories from another life, another timeline. These are echoes of your deeper intelligence and glimpses into a wider spectrum of reality that your brain is already wired to access.

According to Di Biase, your entire nervous system is quantum capable. Cerebrospinal fluid, microtubules, and electromagnetic resonance all serve as conduits for non-local information. In truth, your "sixth sense" and beyond may be your first language, forgotten beneath layers of social conditioning and mental noise.

And here's what's critical to understand: you don't need an AI chip or neural implant to enhance perception. You already have the hardware. What you need is frequency alignment, energetic coherence, and clear intention.

Your DNA operates as the primary antenna, transmitting and receiving information from across dimensions. Your brain is the bridge, a processor translating frequency signals into meaning, perception, and experience.

You are a co-creator of the world through your frequency, your choices, and the resonance of your DNA.

Are You Ready to Activate Your Higher Senses?

As solid as the world may appear, it is a canvas of frequency, perception, and consciousness and you are the artist.

Across cultures and spiritual lineages, the idea that humans possess extraordinary abilities has long been known. In the yogic tradition, these powers are called **Siddhis,** which include faculties such as telepathy, levitation, bi-location, and divine perception, attained through deep meditation and inner purity. Indigenous cultures speak of dream-walkers, visionaries, and shapeshifters; mystics and seers have tuned into higher realms for millennia.

Humans are innately equipped with 12 Higher Sensory Perceptions; each linked to a specific strand of DNA and its corresponding dimensional frequency band. These senses are technologies encoded within your blueprint, awaiting activation. And I've witnessed them firsthand. In one session with a six-year-old boy, his Extra Ocular Vision (EOV) was activated. This is the ability to see without using the physical eyes. After three sessions, he was effortlessly reading a book while wearing a mindfold (a specially designed blindfold that blocks out all light). Children are especially responsive to these activations, as their brains are not yet rigidly patterned by societal conditioning. EOV demonstrates that perception is not confined to the eyes; it's a function of consciousness itself.

Whether through Siddhis, modern quantum models, or your own subtle experiences of "just knowing," these higher senses are real, measurable (in their effect), and profoundly transformative. As your DNA heals and re-coheres, what seems miraculous becomes natural.

Here is a look at the 12 Higher Senses and how they may already be awakening in you.

1. Clairvoyance (Higher Vision)

Associated with 4thdimensional awareness, this ability enables you to see energy fields, auras, light codes, or even interdimensional structures. You may have glimpsed this if you've ever seen flashes of color around someone, perceived movement from the corner of your eye, or had vivid visions in meditation. Children often draw beings or symbols they "see" yet cannot explain.

"When the third eye is opened, one sees the entire universe in oneself and oneself in all beings."— **Patanjali**, *Yoga Sutras, on Divya Drishti*

2. Clairaudience (Higher Hearing)

Linked to 5thdimensional perception, this ability enables you to hear beyond the physical; for example, hearing inner voices, tones, or downloads of information. You might suddenly "hear" a word or phrase when seeking guidance or sense a ringing in your ears that coincides with energetic shifts. Many mediums and sensitives receive messages this way.

"Sound is the first-born of the Absolute... through it, all things were made visible." — **Rig Veda** on *Nada Brahma (the universe is sound)*

3. Clairsentience (Empathic Awareness)

Connected to the 6thdimension, this ability is about feeling others' emotions, sensing the energy of a room, or picking up on subtle shifts in frequency. Empaths live this daily, knowing something is off without explanation. This is what enables them to feel another's physical pain or joy in their own body.

"To feel everything without becoming overwhelmed is the gift of the awakened heart." — **Sufi saying** on the mystic path of heart-based knowing

4. Claircognizance (Instant Knowing)

A 7th dimensional faculty, this enables knowing without knowing how you know. This can show up as sudden insight or unshakable clarity. It's often how visionaries or inventors download complex information seemingly from out of nowhere, like a blueprint landing in the mind fully formed.

"Knowledge is a structure in consciousness that can arise fully formed when the mind is still." — **Maharishi Mahesh Yogi** on *ritambhara prajna (truth-bearing wisdom)*

5. Dimensional Navigation

This ability, activated at the 8th dimensional level, gives you the ability to shift timelines, access parallel versions of self, or leap into higher future potentials. It may appear as déjà vu, reality shifts, or moments of feeling like you're "jumping tracks" in life. Lucid dreamers and timeline shifters access this regularly.

"In the dreamtime, we move across space and time, accessing knowledge beyond the stars." — **Aboriginal Australian teaching** on *multi-dimensional dreaming*

6. Hyperdimensional Awareness

A 9th dimensional activation, this enables a deep knowing that you exist simultaneously across multiple planes. You may begin to sense yourself in meditation as vast, non-local, or aware of other versions of self in different roles or places. This overlaps with what mystics call the Oversoul connection.

"The Oversoul knows neither time nor distance. It contains the memory of all that you have ever been and will be." — **Ralph Waldo Emerson**, *The Over-Soul*

7. Telepathic Reception

Linked to the 10th dimensional fields, this ability enables you to receive messages directly mind-to-mind or heart-to-heart. You might think of someone, and they immediately message you, or feel their thoughts arriving in your own mind. Telepathy also includes animal communication, plant consciousness, and interspecies awareness.

"When the heart is pure, no words are needed. The thought arrives before the sound." — **Taoist teaching** on *mind-to-mind communication*

8. Energetic Projection & Manipulation

Associated with the 11th dimension, this is the ability to influence or construct energetic forms, such as healing with the hands, transmitting light codes, or reshaping outcomes through directed intent. Qi Gong masters, energy healers, and light workers embody this sensory level.

"The one who is established in truth commands energy as easily as breath." - **Theosophical writings** *on mastery of prana and etheric forces*

9. Auric Vision

The ability to see fields of light, symbols, or color around people, objects, or environments available through 12th dimensional activation. You might notice a gold shimmer in meditation, or "see" energetic patterns as part of your intuitive reading. This sense often emerges as inner sight during energy work.

"When the eyes of the soul are opened, light appears not from the sun, but from within."— **Mystic Gnostic text** *on the inner seeing of subtle fields*

10. Bi-Location & Time Travel

Conscious movement through spacetime. This ability enables you to be in two places at once or retrieve information from other times. This may arise in dreams, deep meditation, or real-time awareness of events happening elsewhere. Advanced yogis and mystics report such experiences regularly.

"The yogi whose mind is one-pointed can enter other bodies, visit distant realms, and know past and future time." — **Patanjali**, *Yoga Sutras, on Vibhuti Pada (powers of the mind)*

11. Quantum Sensory Perception

The ability to access the intelligence of the morphogenetic field and tap into the source code of reality. This manifests as being guided by synchronicity or intuitively knowing what's aligned without needing validation. It's the energetic "knowing" behind the scenes.

"The field is the sole governing agency of the particle." — **Albert Einstein** *referring to the primacy of the unified field over matter*

12. Lightbody Integration & Activation

Embodying your multi-dimensional self as light and intelligence. This is the alchemical merging of spirit and matter, when higher senses unify and operate cohesively. You may feel pulses of energy, spontaneous vibrations, or expanded states of bliss and coherence.

"You are not a body that has a soul. You are a soul that wears a body of light."
— **Esoteric Hermetic teaching**, *on the integration of form and essence*

These may seem like curiosities or metaphysical trivia, yet they are evidence that you are a multi-dimensional being navigating a far more fluid and responsive reality than you've been taught.

If your DNA is the receiver of reality, your higher senses are the channels of interpretation. They let you interact with non-local information, receive insight across timelines, and connect deeply with the morphogenetic field.

Sleep: The Portal Between Worlds

Mainstream science tells us that sleep is essential for physical restoration, memory consolidation, and emotional regulation. During sleep, the brain shifts into alternate wave states - theta, delta, and even gamma, epsilon, and lambda; each state is associated with altered consciousness, healing, and deep memory integration. Some emerging thought leaders suggest that this nightly restoration is not just biochemical but also energetic, resonating at the quantum level to reorganize clarity, coherence, and vitality.

Think of your body as a computer. Sleep is the process of dimming the screen but not shutting down the system. In fact, some of your most powerful processing happens in the background, in realms your waking mind can't fully access. Sleep is a gateway to the quantum field, where the filters of linear time, ego, and sensory input are softened, allowing you to traverse dimensions, reconnect with soul fragments, and interact with aspects of your multidimensional self.

Numerous studies show that during REM (Rapid Eye Movement) sleep (a phase when your eyes dart beneath closed lids and your brain activity closely resembles wakefulness), your brain behaves as though you're inside another reality. REM is when vivid dreams, lucid dreaming, and out-of-body experiences (OBEs) most often occur, suggesting that sleep is not a passive state, but an inherently exploratory one. The pineal gland is most active during sleep cycles, hinting at its role as an inner stargate to other realms.

Research from institutions like the Max Planck Institute and Stanford's Sleep Research Center highlight the brain's ability to consolidate and "edit" memory during sleep. Who or what determines what is retained, deleted, or distorted remains an open question.

This brings up an uncomfortable truth: sleep is also when memory is most vulnerable. Dreams can encode insight or distort it entirely, making the night a rich terrain for transformation as well as for rewriting our inner narratives.

Dreams, Memory, and Timeline Insertion

Dreams are more than unconscious processing; they are portals to other timelines, parallel realities, and hidden memories.

Yet, just as dreams can reveal truth, they can also be manipulated. Memory wipes, dream inserts, and distorted recollections are real phenomena, and they occur especially during sleep, trauma, or heightened spiritual work.

Have you ever had a memory of something that you swore really happened, only to find no evidence that it actually had? Or had dreams that felt like downloads, yet left you feeling confused or fragmented?

Practices like dream journaling, shielding, and conscious breathwork help you anchor truth amidst manipulation.

Ancient Wisdom & Modern Rediscovery

Across centuries, cultures, and continents, Mystery Schools emerged as sacred centers for inner transformation where initiates were trained in the deeper laws of the cosmos, human potential, and the hidden architecture of reality.

These esoteric schools were reserved for those ready to undergo initiations of consciousness, often involving strict discipline, symbolic death and rebirth, and practices designed to activate the dormant senses and reawaken the divine blueprint within. Their purpose? To initiate humans into their true multi-dimensional nature.

From the Egyptian Mystery Schools of Heliopolis, Karnak, and Denderah, where initiates studied sacred geometry, alchemy, and cosmic law, to the Vedic Rishis of India, who accessed the Akashic records through deep states of meditation and mantra, to the Taoist sages practicing inner alchemy in mountain retreats to awaken the light body, to the shamans and medicine men and women of indigenous cultures, who used plant medicines, fasting, drumming, and vision quests to access the spirit realms across these traditions, a central truth persisted. Human perception is malleable and can be vastly expanded.

These Mystery Schools held teachings on:

- Energetic anatomy (chakras, nadis, meridians)

- Astro-theology (aligning with celestial cycles)

Expanding Beyond Fiction: The Mystics and Scientists Demonstrating Superhuman Abilities

While many still associate "superhuman abilities" with science fiction, there are individuals today actively demonstrating them. Researchers and mystics such as Ernst Veter, Alex Shymko, and others are proving that walking on water, traversing timelines, and hyperdimensional jumping are not merely the stuff of myths, but real, tangible skills that can be cultivated.

• Ernst Veter has explored the mechanics of quantum jumping and navigating parallel dimensions, shedding light on how consciousness itself is the key to bending space and time.

• Alex Shymko has extensively studied human teleportation and heightened bio-energetic abilities, proposing that certain states of consciousness allow access to higher-dimensional movement.

• Mystics and sages across traditions have long spoken of levitation, bilocation, and spontaneous healing as natural extensions of human potential rather than supernatural anomalies.

These abilities are often relegated to science fiction or comic books, yet they are part of our true multi-dimensional nature, waiting to be reclaimed.

- Symbolic language and sacred codes

- Life after death and reincarnation

- Direct communion with non-physical beings or intelligence

- Practices to access clairvoyance, healing, prophecy, and higher guidance

The initiate's journey was one of *self-mastery*, moving from ignorance and separation into gnosis, remembrance, and full embodiment of one's divine essence.

However, with time, many of these teachings were hidden, distorted, or destroyed. Religious and political institutions seeking to control society labeled such wisdom heretical or dangerous. Knowledge that once empowered individuals to commune with Source directly was replaced with dogma, fear, and disempowerment.

The Industrial Age, with its mechanistic empirical lens, further suppressed the mystical, reducing consciousness to brain activity and spiritual reality to superstition. The mystical was divorced from the materialist view of science.

Yet truth has a way of resurfacing.

Today, there is a renaissance of the ancient ways. As quantum physics and consciousness studies reveal the non-local, energetic nature of reality, what was once considered *esoteric* is now being validated as *essential*.

Modern expressions of Mystery Schools and initiatory paths exist all around us:

- The Rosicrucians, who preserve Hermetic and mystical Christian teachings

- The Kabbalists, exploring the Tree of Life as a map of consciousness

- The Freemasons, inheritors of ancient architectural and spiritual codes

- The Anthroposophical movement, birthed from Rudolf Steiner's clairvoyant insights

- The Theosophical Society, bridging science, ancient wisdom, and modern esotericism

- And many new schools of metaphysics, energy medicine, and multi-dimensional training emerging across the globe

Even ancient lineages like the Andean Q'ero, the Egyptian Khemit School, or Tibetan Bon practitioners continue to pass down initiations, often in secrecy.

These teachings are resurfacing because humanity is ready. People everywhere are remembering who they are as multi-dimensional creators capable of perceiving, healing, and co-creating reality through frequency and intention.

You are the modern initiate, and this time, the temple is within.

The Future of Perception: A Cinematic Leap

Imagine a world where children are taught to trust their intuition as much as mathematics. Where communication happens not just with words, but with frequencies of feeling and resonance. Where cities are designed around energetic harmony, and healing is a process of remembering one's original blueprint.

Training Your Multi-Dimensional Senses

To awaken and refine Higher Sensory Perception, you must first deprogram the limitations imposed by societal conditioning. The following methods can enhance your ability to perceive beyond the five senses:

- **Shifting States of Consciousness.** Regular meditation, breathwork, and lucid dreaming practices help access deeper layers of perception.

- **Sensory Deprivation & Enhancement.** Time in darkness, silence, or floatation tanks can amplify perception by removing external distractions.

- **Decoding Symbols & Energetic Patterns.** Learning to interpret synchronicities, dreams, and non-verbal cues enhances perception.

- **The Power of Attention & Focus.** Intentional awareness of subtle shifts in energy and emotion strengthens sensitivity.

- **Energetic Hygiene & Detox.** Reducing exposure to toxins, electromagnetic pollution, and processed foods helps clear the body for refined perception.

In this future, Higher Sensory Perception is the standard. Humanity no longer perceives reality as flat and finite but as layered, holographic, and alive with intelligence. There is no need for machines to extend your mind because you are the technology.

Mystics, scientists, and visionaries converge. The lines between biology and light blur. Telepathy becomes more natural than texting. Instead of virtual reality, you engage with the frequency of reality, shifting timelines with intention and sensing multi-dimensional fields with ease.

In this world, perception is creative. Each thought is a brushstroke, and each frequency, a thread in the living tapestry of existence.

INTEGRATION KEYS
Higher Sensory Perception: Accessing the Unseen

- Higher Sensory Perception (HSP) is a natural capacity encoded in the multi-dimensional architecture of all human beings. These senses allow access to non-local information, energetic patterns, and interdimensional communication.

- As you activate Multi-Dimensional Intelligence, your perception begins to stretch beyond the five-sense model. You start to register frequency signatures, energetic imprints, subtle emotional cues, and timeline fluctuations with increasing clarity and coherence.

- Multi-Dimensional Intelligence reminds you that HSP develops not through force, but through refinement, and by clearing energetic density, stilling the mind, and attuning to your field. The quieter your inner world, the more precise your extrasensory data becomes.

- Many experience these senses through imagery, tones, geometric codes, or inner knowing. As trust in these impressions grows, your multi-dimensional interface sharpens. You move from passive sensing to active interfacing with fields, beings, timelines, and frequencies beyond conventional perception.

- HSP is a vital strand of Multi-Dimensional Intelligence. It enhances intuitive decision-making, enables resonance-based alignment, and supports your evolution from reactive to responsive, from blindness to vision, and from limitation to multi-dimensional mastery.

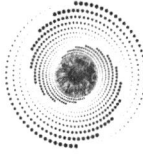

Chapter Six

Energy Coherence: The Engine of Embodied Multi-Dimensionality

Introduction

The Coherence Imperative: Awakening Without Fragmentation

For many, the journey into expanded states of consciousness can be likened to a seismic influx; a floodgate of energy that bursts open, overwhelming the circuits of body and mind. Whether triggered by kundalini activations, deep meditation, near-death experiences, plant medicine journeys, or exposure to high-frequency fields, this awakening initiates a process that is both electrifying and destabilizing.

In these moments, the human system becomes like a complex circuit board or vibrational tuning fork, and one that must recalibrate to receive and integrate new bandwidths of reality. Without proper alignment, it shorts out, surges, or fragments. And just like detoxing the physical body can produce a Herxheimer reaction (commonly known as herxing, where symptoms temporarily worsen as toxins are expelled), the energetic body too can go into turbulence as distortions, traumas, and unintegrated fragments rise to the surface for release.

This is energetic fact.

What appears as chaos, disorientation, fatigue, or emotional overwhelm is often a sign that the old architecture of self is dissolving to make space for a more coherent multi-dimensional embodiment. Yet few are prepared for this phase of the process, and even fewer are taught how to stabilize their field, refine their frequency, or anchor higher intelligence without becoming energetically fragmented.

Tom Kenyon, one of the most well-known sound healers of our time, experienced his first dramatic shift into heightened awareness while still in university. In his early twenties, an intense and spontaneous kundalini activation overwhelmed his system, leaving him disoriented, flooded with expanded perception, and barely able to function in the physical world. The episode was so destabilizing that he reportedly staggered to the hospital, unable to make sense of the altered states rushing through his body and mind. It was through the discovery of vocal toning and sound resonance that he found a way to stabilize his awareness by using sound as a bridge to coherence, much like tuning an instrument to harmonize with a greater symphony of frequencies.

Similarly, my own experience after completing a breatharian and dry fasting retreat, led to a sudden influx of multi-dimensional awareness. I became acutely attuned to subtle energies and expanded perceptions. While the clarity and insights were extraordinary, the energetic intensity was equally destabilizing. Without the integration tools and internal coherence I had cultivated, the experience could have become overwhelming.

This is a common pattern for those who undergo spontaneous or accelerated spiritual activations. Some are propelled into states of bliss and heightened insight. Others are plunged into emotional turbulence, anxiety, confusion, or even a sense of detachment from reality. These aren't "symptoms" in a pathological sense; rather they are signs of a system trying to run upgraded software without the proper operating structure in place.

The same applies to those who engage in plant medicine journeys. Substances such as Ayahuasca, Yopo, or Bufo catapult consciousness into multi-dimensional realities, often bypassing the natural energetic safeguards of the lower fields. Without proper integration, these intense experiences can shatter or fragment the energetic system, leaving individuals vulnerable, disoriented, or psychically destabilized. This is why a level of inner maturity, strong energetic grounding, and guided support during the integration period is essential. These gateways open very real doors, and what you meet on the other side depends greatly on how well your system is prepared to receive and integrate expanded perception.

Francisco Di Biase's concept of a *holoinformational universe* offers a profound context for this. You exist within a self-organizing, intelligent field, an ocean of non-local quantum information from which consciousness is continuously emerging and evolving. This "plenum" is not empty; it is encoded with cosmic DNA, in-formation with purpose and pattern. But when the human system lacks coherence, it cannot properly decode or embody this information. Like trying to download a high-frequency program into outdated hardware, the result is often energetic chaos, emotional fragmentation, or perceptual overload.

Energy coherence, then, is not optional. It is imperative. It is the stabilizing matrix that allows you to interface with higher frequencies of intelligence without collapsing your nervous system, distorting your perception, or fragmenting your sense of self.

KEY QUESTIONS FOR EXPLORATION IN CHAPTER SIX

◊   What if chaos is a signal that your system is reconfiguring to hold more of your multi-dimensional self?

◊   What outdated structures in your mind, body, or identity are ready to dissolve, making space for higher coherence?

◊   Are you ready to transmit clarity, presence, and truth consistently across timelines and realities?

From Chaos to Coherence: The Science of Order Within Complexity

Ilya Prigogine, Nobel Prize-winning physicist and chemist, introduced a revolutionary concept that forever changed how transformation was understood. In his theory of dissipative structures, Prigogine showed that when complex systems are pushed far from equilibrium, they undergo instability and chaotic fluctuations, breakdowns, or unpredictable patterns. Yet paradoxically, this temporary disorder is not the end. It is the threshold.

Out of these fluctuations, a new structure emerges, more ordered, more coherent, and more complex than before. Prigogine called this process "order through fluctuation." In other words, breakdown leads to breakthrough. Collapse leads to coherence.

This principle applies to chemical systems, planetary dynamics, and it applies to you. In fact, it applies to every human who has stood on the precipice of awakening and felt like their life, body, or mind was unraveling.

Emotional turbulence, energetic surges, brain fog, hypersensitivity, extreme fatigue, spiritual euphoria followed by despair; these symptoms of overwhelm can be understood through the lens of dissipative dynamics. When you enter expanded states of consciousness, you become an energetic system operating outside of your previous equilibrium. Old identity patterns destabilize. Neural pathways rewire. Brainwave activity shifts. Emotional memory surfaces.

Physical, emotional, and psychic toxins release. You become, for a time, chaotic.

Just as a system undergoing a frequency shift in cymatics becomes disordered before snapping into a higher geometric resonance, so too does the human energy field destabilize before forming a new multi-dimensional coherence. The "mess" is the message. The disorder is the doorway.

From a thermodynamic perspective, these spiritual initiations can be seen as dissipative processes where the human energy field is shedding entropy, detoxing what no longer resonates, and preparing to anchor more refined frequencies of order. The more complex the consciousness being birthed, the greater the instability threshold that must be crossed.

This is why awakening can feel like both death and rebirth. The old coherence dissolves, and in its place, a higher form takes shape.

This threshold is like the moment a glass holding water shatters. The water, once confined, now flows freely. It can no longer return to its previous container. If the boundaries of the self, including beliefs, habits and identities, are like the glass, then once these limitations break through a state of flux, what emerges is fluid, expansive, and uncontainable.

This echoes a powerful internal process that I've found powerful and effective while working with clients. Seemingly conflicting aspects of the self are brought into harmony through the dissolution of the inner boundaries that sustain the conflict. When these boundaries soften, a deeper intelligence takes over. Integration occurs naturally. Rather than being solved, the "problem" dissolves, because the container that held the tension no longer exists in the same form. What once felt divided is now experienced as whole.

When the glass breaks, there is no need to mourn the shards. The focus shifts to the water which is finally free to flow farther than ever before. Amid transformation, fluctuations are inevitable. They also carry the potential for profound reorganization if you allow yourself to ride their rhythm.

The Rhythms of Inner Order: Central Axis, Heart, Brain, and the Spirit Gateway

If coherence is the architecture of consciousness, then rhythm is its pulse.

Our body is more than a physical organism; it is a living quantum interface. While the heart and brain maintain electromagnetic balance and perceptual coherence, there exists a higher control point, a central access gate that links your multi-dimensional self to Source.

This gateway is known in inner science as the Central Axis.

Located between the heart and throat centers, the Central Axis point acts as a multi-dimensional zero-point, the node where life force, consciousness currents, and your higher identity codes converge. It's more than a chakra. It is the origin point of individuation, where the current of Spirit steps down into your bioenergetic field. When the Central Axis is coherent and active, it allows you to regulate perception, frequency, and energy flow across dimensions with clarity and precision. From this Central Axis radiate three living streams of intelligent light:

- Vital Light: Subtle energy units that weave through the light-body and animate your biology with living intelligence.

- Source Spark: The ignition impulse from Source and a flash of divine will that awakens awareness into form.

- Spirit Matrix: The energetic zone of your Spirit Body that stores con-sciousness and the sacred geometry of your soul's blueprint.

The **Spirit Body**, often conflated with the soul, is something distinct. The soul represents the *experiencer-self*, the aspect of you collecting incarnational memory; the Spirit Body is the *eternal witness*, the aspect of Source expressing as you across time, space, and density. It is through the Spirit Body that the Central Axis communicates, translating high-frequency intelligence into energetic instruction for your form identity.

When this Central Axis is blocked, reversed, or dormant, the heart and brain struggle to maintain coherence. Energy becomes scattered and the field is open to intrusion or fragmentation. When the Central Axis is active and integrated, the heart's rhythm harmonizes, the brainwaves entrain into coherence, and the multi-dimensional self clicks into alignment like tuning forks resonating across octaves of light.

Multi-Dimensional Coherence Begins at the Core

It's easy to believe that the heart is the master regulator, and in many respects, it is the conductor of emotional and physiological harmony. But true multi-dimensional coherence must arise from the core, from the zero-point flame within the Central Axis.

The heart responds to the Central Axis directives. The brain entrains to the heart's field, and the body aligns when all three are in harmonic synergy.

This is why so many spiritual paths begin with stillness, not just to calm the mind, but to re-enter the center point of inner creation. In silence, the quantum spark can be felt, the Spirit Body can speak, and from that center, coherence is remembered.

Tuning the Temple: The Hidden Power of Sound, Frequency, and Harmonic Coherence

In the beginning was the Word, not a word spoken, but a frequency formedSound is not just vibration and oscilltion. It is instruction, pattern, memory, and activation.Every cell in your body listens. Every strand of your DNA is attuned to its own harmonic blueprint. When you speak, tone, chant, or sing, as well as making sound, you are vibrating and oscillating reality into being. You are tuning the temple of your multi-dimensional self.

Cellular memory refers to the phenomenon where experiences, especially traumatic or highly charged ones, are encoded in the brain, tissues, muscles, fascia, and even in the DNA of the body. These imprints operate like unconscious programs, looping old patterns and emotional signatures beneath conscious awareness. Each cell becomes a resonator of past experience, shaping perception and behavior long after the originating event. When sound is used consciously through pure tones, sacred music, harmonic breath, or intentional silence, it becomes a carrier wave capable of reorganizing these hidden imprints.

The science of cymatics, as mentioned earlier, has demonstrated that sound organizes matter. When a surface sprinkled with particles is subjected to vibration, it forms intricate geometric patterns, each unique to the frequency used. A slight shift in frequency causes the particles to dissolve into chaos until a new pattern emerges. This is what happens to you during frequency shifts, multi-dimensional awakenings, and energetic recalibration. Cellular echoes may rise as memories as well as sensations, dreams, or spontaneous emotional waves. This is recalibration. The intelligence of the body begins to rewrite the past in real time, not through thought, but through frequency.

Releasing cellular memory is about restoring resonance, reharmonizing the signal and remembering the original template before distortion. Through sound, you're both healing and remembering yourself into coherence.

The Hijacking of Harmonics

Sadly, not all sound heals. Some sound distorts.

At a certain point in recent history, which many trace to World War II or the mid-20th century, there was a deliberate global shift in musical tuning. The standard concert pitch was changed from a frequency of 432 Hertz (Hz), a frequency aligned with the Earth's natural resonance and geometry, to 440Hz. This might seem like a minor difference, yet the implications are vast.

Researchers, and authors such as Mark Devlin (*Musical Truths*) and Preston Nichols (*The Music of Time*), argue that this pitch change was not a neutral decision, but a form of frequency-based programming intended to unbalance the human energy field, fragment emotional resonance, and disrupt connection to Source harmonics.

The frequency of 440Hz has been shown to agitate the nervous system, overstimulate the left brain, and subtly create dissonance in the energy field. By contrast, 432Hz soothes, aligns, and entrains your brainwaves and energy field into a more harmonious and coherent state. In fact, this frequency is said to mirror the rhythm of the Earth's Schumann resonance and the human body's own biofield. Musical performances tuned to 432Hz, such as classical compositions by Verdi, or modern ambient healing tracks, have been observed to slow the heart rate, reduce anxiety, and create feelings of spaciousness, stillness, and unity. Many ancient instruments, including Tibetan singing bowls and Indigenous flutes, naturally vibrate closer to 432Hz.

The frequency of this music feels different, as it is easier to harmonize with it vibrationally.

This change in pitch was not the only distortion. Tuning systems, tonal structures, and rhythmic entrainment have also been manipulated to dull consciousness and disconnect individuals from their internal guidance systems. Many modern pop music structures embed loops and beats that induce fragmentation rather than promote flow.

Restoring Harmonic Coherence

Sound is an effective and easily accessible tool for stabilizing the Central Axis, activating the Spirit Body, and realigning to your multi-dimensional intelligence.

Consider these coherence-restoring tools:

• **Vocal Toning**. The human voice is the most direct transmitter of Spirit energy through matter. Toning the vowel sounds (A, E, I, O, U) with intention through the chest, throat, and cranium activates specific energy centers. Toning into the Central Axis field creates a resonance chamber for Spirit intelligence to flow more clearly.

• **432Hz & 528Hz Frequencies**. Tones at these frequencies help repair DNA, soften emotional contraction, and entrain the field to natural coherence. 528Hz, known as the "Miracle Frequency," has been linked to heart opening and cellular regeneration.

• **Binaural Beats & Harmonic Overtones**. Listening to slightly detuned frequencies through both ears allows the brain to entrain to a third "phantom frequency." This creates alpha, theta, or gamma brain wave states that stabilize multi-dimensional perception and access inner guidance.

• **Chanting & Mantra**. Mantras are spiritual affirmations as well as passwords for accessing higher states of consciousness. Each syllable carries sonic encoding aligned to dimensional bandwidths. Even simple chants like "OM" or "HU" act as frequency carriers into the stillpoint.

• **Shofar (Sacred Horn)**. Used for millennia in Judaic traditions, the Shofar–a ram's horn–is far more than a ceremonial trumpet. It is a primal instrument of awakening. The unique

For the binaural effect to work properly, the delivery method matters. Earbuds, while convenient, often sit outside or shallowly in the ear canal. They can leak sound, miss deeper overtones, and fail to deliver the full stereo separation required for true binaural entrainment. By contrast, closed-back, over-ear headphones create an immersive sound chamber around the ears. They offer better spatial separation, deeper bass response, and clearer harmonic layering, which are essential for activating the brain's natural synchrony with layered frequencies.

If you're using sound as a tool for consciousness exploration, the hardware you choose isn't trivial, it can be the difference between surface relaxation and a truly altered state.

frequencies it produces are said to cut through layers of density, collapse distortions in the energy field, and initiate spiritual clarity. Some mystics describe the Shofar's blast as a "sonic scalpel" that slices through veils of illusion, restoring direct connection with Source. It does not play a melody but issues a raw, elemental vibration that speaks to the soul's remembrance. Each blast acts as a reset signal to the bioenergetic system, especially effective during transitional thresholds, such as new cycles, deep cleanses, or DNA upgrades.

When applied consistently, sound becomes a self-retuning system, clearing distortions, releasing energetic toxins, and supporting the field through spiritual upgrades or detox phases.

Brainwave Synchronization and Higher States of Awareness

Brainwave coherence is another key aspect of stabilizing multi-dimensional awareness. Different brainwave states; namely, alpha, theta, delta, gamma, epsilon, and lambda, play specific roles in perception, cognition, and spiritual experience.

But let us not forget the starting point for most: **Beta Waves**.

• **Beta Waves (14-30 Hz):** Beta is the brain's default waking state where you are alert, analytical, and engaged with the external world. While essential for focused thinking and task execution, prolonged beta activity, especially the high-beta range, is associated with stress, anxiety, and hypervigilance. In today's world, constant stimulation from smart devices, social media, and environmental noise traps many individuals in chronic beta activation. This sustained alertness hard-wires the brain into the sympathetic nervous system, your fight-or-flight mode. Over time, this creates energetic incoherence, reduces access to higher states, and disrupts the natural rhythms of the body and mind.

Interestingly, visual focus plays a significant role in determining brainwave states. *Foveal vision*, a narrow, focused gaze, often used when looking at screens or concentrating intently, is directly linked to beta brainwave activity and the sympathetic stress response. In contrast, *peripheral vision* - the soft, unfocused awareness of the space around you - automatically triggers the parasympathetic nervous system, associated with calm, restoration, and healing. Peripheral vision invites the brain into alpha waves, enabling relaxed alertness, enhanced sensory perception, and a deeper connection to the present moment.

In this way, something as simple as shifting visual awareness can serve as a powerful tool for accessing altered states of consciousness. By expanding awareness to include peripheral space, you can interrupt stress patterns and open the gateway to alpha and beyond.

• **Alpha Waves (8–14 Hz):**

Alpha waves are associated with relaxed focus, creativity, and a state of wakeful rest. When in alpha, your experiences a sense of calm clarity, often linked to meditative states and creative problem-solving. Alpha waves are the bridge between conscious thought and unconscious processing, allowing intuition to flow more freely.

• **Theta Waves (4–8 Hz):** Theta waves emerge during deep relaxation, meditation, and the hypnagogic state between wakefulness and sleep. They are strongly linked to intuition, memory recall, and accessing unconscious information. Many people report vivid imagery, spontaneous insights, and deep emotional healing while in theta states. Shamans, healers, and advanced meditators often operate in theta to access higher guidance.

• **Delta Waves (0.5–4 Hz):** Delta waves are the slowest brainwaves and are dominant during deep sleep and states of deep, unconscious healing. This frequency is linked to cellular regeneration, immune system function, and non-verbal collective awareness. For most people, Delta is only accessible during the deepest stages of sleep. However, advanced mystics, yogis, and Tibetan monks have demonstrated the ability to remain conscious while entering Delta states, a neurological feat that allows the body to rest deeply while awareness expands beyond the physical.

There are accounts of Himalayan yogis in these ultra-slow wave states who can perceive objects behind walls, sense events in distant locations, or merge their awareness with the field of all life. One such case, documented in yogic oral traditions, describes a sadhu who would sit in meditation beneath a tree and answer questions about events occurring miles away, accurately describing people's movements, conversations, and hidden objects. When tested, he was found to be in an extremely slow brainwave pattern, more commonly associated with dreamless sleep.

In Delta, the individual identity softens, the ego recedes, and perception no longer relies on physical senses. You begin to sense through frequency, not form.

• **Gamma Waves (40+ Hz):** Gamma waves, the highest frequency brainwaves, are linked to heightened perception, expanded consciousness, and deep integration of information across the brain. These waves are associated with peak mental performance, lucid awareness, and moments of unity consciousness. In laboratory studies using EEG and other brain-imaging technology, Tibetan monks and seasoned meditators have been recorded while producing intense bursts of gamma brainwave activity during states of deep, unwavering focus and transcendental absorption.

You may have experienced gamma without realizing it. For example, in moments of total immersion where time disappears and you become at one, or in flow, with the task or experience. You could find yourself in the flow while painting, dancing, or writing. Hours pass like minutes, and you're flooded with insight, clarity, and creativity. Or during a moment of awe in nature, when the boundaries between you and the world dissolve into stillness, yet your mind feels incredibly alive and alert. In these moments, your brain isn't relaxed, it's synchronized. Multiple regions are firing in harmony, forming a unified field of awareness.

Gamma is a heightened focus and the integration of intellect and intuition, matter and spirit, perception and presence.

• **Epsilon Waves (<0.5 Hz):** Epsilon waves, even slower than delta, are associated with extreme states of inner stillness and non-dual awareness. In this state, the body may appear lifeless with the breath and heartbeat nearly undetectable, yet awareness remains fully awake. This brainwave pattern has been observed in advanced yogis, monks, and adepts who have practiced deep, sustained meditation over many years. These are the states where cellular regeneration, timeless awareness, and subtle body activation become possible. Some traditions describe this as the "ground of all being," a return to Source consciousness prior to form. Epsilon states have been linked to the phenomenon of the Tibetan Rainbow Body, where accomplished practitioners dematerialize at the time of death, leaving behind only nails or hair. The body, having fully transmuted into light, no longer follows the rules of linear decay.

• **Lambda Waves (100+ Hz):** Lambda waves, on the other end of the spectrum, represent the highest known frequencies of conscious brain activity. They are correlated with heightened spiritual ecstasy, out-of-body experiences, teleportation phenomena, and multi-dimensional perception. These waves have been recorded in individuals experiencing expanded unity states, such as merging with cosmic consciousness or being aware of multiple realities simultaneously. Interestingly, lambda and epsilon appear to operate in synergy with the fastest and slowest brainwaves forming a harmonic loop. This dynamic tension creates a unique neurological state where profound stillness (epsilon) and heightened awareness (lambda) co-exist. This may explain how advanced mystics can appear motionless externally while inwardly navigating vast dimensional landscapes or entering samadhi states that transcend time and space.

Together, Epsilon and Lambda waves point to the next frontier of human consciousness. By training the brain to enter these states consistently, you strengthen your ability to navigate multi-dimensional intelligence with stability and precision. And by understanding the visual and neurological links between stress and stillness, you gain access to subtle tools that help shift your frequency moment by moment, breath by breath.

Detox, Frequency Shifts, and Emotional Release

Sometimes, as the field attunes to new frequencies, emotional residues surface. Grief, rage, fatigue, or sadness may arise as signals that older embedded programs are being released. This is the energetic purge before harmonic renewal; just like sand scattering before it reorganizes into a new geometry, as demonstrated in cymatic experiments.

The Light Within: Bio-Photonic Emissions and the Luminous Energy Field

If sound sculpts reality, then light reveals its blueprint.

Every cell in your body emits light, an invisible glow of ultra-weak photons known as bio-photons. This light is not merely a byproduct of cellular metabolism. It is an expression of intelligence. It pulses with coherence, rhythm, and communication. In fact, your entire energy field (the aura) can be understood as a luminous interface of consciousness and biology, radiating and receiving information through light.

Coherent Light = Coherent Life

Dr. Fritz-Albert Popp, a pioneering biophysicist, discovered that healthy cells emit coherent light that is structured, harmonious, and rhythmic. In contrast, diseased or stressed cells produce incoherent, chaotic emissions, like static interrupting a broadcast.

What Popp found is astounding: This biophotonic light acts as a communication network for the body. It coordinates cellular function, regulates DNA expression, and transmits information faster than neural signals. In essence, you are living in a light field, constantly broadcasting and receiving energetic instructions.

Practices such as breathwork, meditation, fasting, and toning were shown to increase the coherence and intensity of this light. Conversely, environmental toxins, processed foods, stress, and electromagnetic overload dim the field, creating energetic static or fragmentation.

With technologies such as Gas Discharge Visualization (GDV), developed by Dr. Konstantin Korotkov, these emissions can be visually mapped. The resulting images often show brilliant, symmetrical halos around those in deep meditation or healing states, and fractured, dim, or unstable fields in those under emotional or physical stress.

Your Energy Field as a Living Light Matrix

The aura is a living matrix that is dynamic, responsive, and multi-dimensional. It reflects your thoughts, emotions, physical vitality, and spiritual alignment in real time. At every moment, your auric field is broadcasting frequencies and receiving data from the environments, timelines, and consciousness fields around you.

As your energy becomes more coherent, your field transforms. The quality of light sharpens, and symmetry increases. The structure becomes more crystalline, geometric, and organized.

Researchers have demonstrated how the biofield can be scanned and read through quantum and frequency-based technologies. This work reveals that disturbances, traumas, and unresolved emotional signatures often appear in the energy field long before they manifest in the body. Using tools like The Genius Insight App, NES Health, Healy, The RASHA, or GDV (Gas Discharge Visualization) technology, practitioners can detect subtle imbalances and then apply targeted frequencies or informational remedies to restore coherence. These systems offer a glimpse into the holographic nature of the human being; the aura not only holds the record of past disruptions, but also the blueprint for healing and resolution.

Biophysicist Dr. James Oschman describes the human body as a *"living matrix"*; a highly conductive, fascia-based network that stores, transmits, and responds to energy. His work in *Energy Medicine: The Scientific Basis*, offers a bridge between quantum biology and healing arts. He demonstrates how touch, frequency, light, and intention can restore order at the cellular level by re-establishing electromagnetic coherence in the body's tissues. Ancient healing systems are validated by looking through the lens of modern biophysics: energy is structural, electrical, and deeply intelligent.

> *"Energy is the currency of life. All healing is, at its foundation, the restoration of the body's electromagnetic order."*
>
> —Dr. James Oschman

This is why coherent individuals can walk into a room and shift the energy of the entire space. Their auric field entrains the environment like a tuning fork resonating in harmony with its surroundings. This is quantum coherence, a bio-photonic emission of structured information that others unconsciously attune to.

Your aura is also your filter. It determines which timelines you access, which beings you interface with, and what experiences you attract. It filters multi-dimensional data, decoding frequencies into thoughts, sensations, and intuitive impressions. The more coherent your field, the clearer your signal, and the greater your access to higher perception, healing, and manifestation.

This is your biological light technology, refined.

Signs of Auric Coherence vs. Distortion

Understanding Your Field as Frequency Technology

Aspect	Coherent Aura	Distorted Aura
Shape	Spherical, symmetrical, spacious	Jagged, collapsed, uneven edges
Color Clarity	Vivid, radiant, high-frequency hues	Dull, murky, or stagnant tones
Emotional Field	Calm, clear, emotionally resonant	Reactive, clouded, residual emotional imprints
Energetic Response	Uplifts and stabilizes others nearby	Drains energy or creates dissonance in environments
Perception & Intuition	Expansive, multi-sensory, receives downloads easily	Foggy, blocked, prone to confusion or outside influence
Magnetism	Attracts synchronicity, clarity, aligned opportunities	Pulls in repetition loops, drama, and misalignment

Seeing the Invisible: Kirlian Photography and Beyond

Long before bio-photon science entered the mainstream, Kirlian photography offered early glimpses into the energy body, as we've seen earlier. This method, developed in 1939 by Semyon Kirlian, captured the corona discharge around living beings, a ghostly light signature that shifted with mood, intention, or health.

While controversial at the time, Kirlian photography hinted that the subtle body is visible to those who know how to look.

Today, with filtered lenses and specific dyes such as the elusive Dicyanin, some claim to perceive energy fields, auras, and even interdimensional beings. I personally own a pair of aura glasses and often take them hiking. The colors in nature become absolutely astounding, almost otherworldly, and the longer you wear them, the richer and more radiant your world becomes. Whether through high-tech optics, frequency-based devices, or simply enhanced inner perception, these tools remind us that the visible spectrum is only a narrow slice of reality. Just beyond our usual sensory bandwidth lies a vibrational world that most have been conditioned not to see.

In fact, with training and coherence, many people naturally develop the ability to see *auras*. This occurs when expanded sensory perception is attuned to a wider light bandwidth.

The Mystery of Dicyanin Dye

Dicyanin dye, once used in early aura goggles, is shrouded in mystery. Originally employed in scientific photography to expand the visible spectrum, it was said to allow users to perceive subtle energy fields or even beings outside the normal range of vision. Rumors persist that Dicyanin was classified by the U.S. government due to its unusual effects on consciousness and perception. While mainstream science dismisses these claims, interest in Dicyanin has not disappeared, especially among those exploring consciousness, auras, and multi-dimensional realities. Whether legend or lost technology, it remains a symbol of how much remains hidden just beyond our visible sight.

Light as a Language of Spirit

From a multi-dimensional intelligence perspective, bio-photons are information carrying memory, pattern, and meaning. They are the whispers of the Spirit Body translated into cellular language.

Light is both a wave and a carrier of consciousness —a "cosmic DNA" transmitting meaning across space-time. In this view, your light field is the broadcast station of your being, emanating your current frequency while receiving upgrades, instructions, and signals from the unified quantum field.

Just as coherence in light reveals the embodiment of higher harmonics in the body, the architecture of your energetic system must also be considered through this expanded lens. The traditional model of seven chakras offers only a partial view and an entry point into a far more complex, multi-dimensional interface. To fully understand how light codes interface with consciousness, must be explored.

The Twelve Chakras (and beyond): Reclaiming the Full Template

Most people are familiar with the traditional seven chakras extending from root to crown; spinning wheels of energy that govern different aspects of human experience. This is only the surface level. The chakra system, like consciousness itself, is multi-dimensional. It extends far beyond the body, beyond even linear time, functioning as a scalar interface that links the physical, emotional, mental, soul, and spirit bodies.

However, each chakra is more than a wheel of energy. It is a quantum portal and a living code that opens access to specific dimensions, timelines, and layers of identity. Just as the nervous system carries information throughout the physical body, the chakra system carries light, sound, memory and intention throughout your multi-dimensional self.

The human body was originally designed to operate with at least 12 active chakra centers, aligned with a 12-strand DNA template and corresponding to 12 dimensions of reality.

These include:

- Chakras 8–12, located above the crown, which govern higher aspects of self: Soul Matrix, Oversoul, Avatar Self, Rishi, and Eckatic levels of identity (the highest spiritual strata of individuality, where one's personal consciousness reunites with Source essence).

- Chakras 13–15, which connect into planetary, galactic, and universal consciousness grids

These upper centers regulate frequency access to higher intelligence, memory fields, and the multi-dimensional structures of the Spirit Body. They are often dormant in most humans due to genetic distortions, trauma patterns, and planetary frequency limitations. They can be reawakened through inner coherence, sound codes, breath, and deep soul work.

Each chakra functions as a scalar vortex, akin to a torsion field that spirals energy in and out of dimensional layers. Far from being simple spinning discs aligned along the spine, chakras operate as sophisticated bi-directional gateways modulating interdimensional current across physical, emotional, mental, and spiritual planes.

Looking through the lenses of quantum bioenergetics and scalar field physics, a healthy chakra doesn't spin in just one direction. Instead, it oscillates with harmonic coherence, rotating simultaneously in two directions ($33^{1/3}$ clockwise and $11^{2/3}$ counterclockwise). This precise ratio forms a scalar standing wave, enabling the chakra to maintain energetic integrity while functioning as a translator of Light-Sound instruction sets from higher-dimensional matrices. One spin vector acts as a magnetic receiver; the other, as an electric transmitter. Together, they create a toroidal feedback loop that sustains consciousness embodiment across timelines and frequency bands.

This principle has been embodied and practiced throughout sacred traditions; most notably, by the whirling dervishes of the Mevlevi Sufi path. As they spin, their right hand is raised to receive Divine current, while their left hand is turned downward to transmit it into the Earth. This movement is more than a dance; it is a ritualized expression of scalar vortex dynamics in motion. The whirling body generates a torsion field through the heart center, mirroring the bi-directional spin of the chakra system and facilitating altered states of consciousness and communion with Source.

In this way, the human chakra system is not limited to the linear "root-to-crown" narrative. It is a multi-dimensional scalar interface, and a living architecture designed to anchor Divine intelligence into form, just as the dervish becomes a living spiral embodying the union of Heaven and Earth.

Imagine your body as a sacred spiral temple. Each chakra, not as a static room but a vortex doorway, spinning in both directions like the twin spirals carved in stone on ancient temples. These spinning gateways keep the temple alive, and they let in light from the heavens and ground wisdom from the Earth.

The clockwise spin is like the sun's spiral radiating outward, expressing, projecting, and creating. The counterclockwise spin is like the spiral of a galaxy drawing in starlight, receiving, remembering and recalibrating.

When in balance, the temple hums in harmonic resonance, much like the whirling dervish, who dances through the architecture of space and time. With one hand reaching up and one down, he becomes the living temple, with his spin generating a toroidal field that bridges worlds.

Chakra Distortion and Energetic Programming

Many people operate with a distorted, fragmented, inverted, or artificially capped chakra system.

For example:

- The base chakra (root) is often embedded with survival programming or fear codes.

- The solar plexus may carry control patterns or ancestral trauma.

- The third eye can be clouded by external thought forms, limiting true inner vision.

Activating the Higher Chakra Fields

Practices for activating and integrating the expanded chakra system include:

- Toning into each center using vowel sounds or harmonic frequencies

- Visualizing the color and geometry of each chakra, not just in the body, but extending beyond it

- Breathwork protocols that spiral energy up through the vertical column

- Spiral codes and light-symbol techniques (when consciously integrated) to anchor higher dimensional energies

- Interfacing with the Central Axis as the central node that modulates frequency into all other centers

When these centers are balanced and aligned, and when spin ratios are restored to their natural configuration you feel better. You become a stabilized conduit for Spirit intelligence, capable of transmitting coherence into any environment. You become the bridge between dimensions and a living portal.

Some of these distortions are inherited epigenetically, meaning the patterns are passed down through changes in gene expression influenced by ancestral experiences, rather than changes to the genetic code itself. Others are the result of social and environmental conditioning, EMF interference, dietary toxicity, or collective fear matrices. In extreme cases, chakra systems may be intentionally manipulated through distorted belief systems, mass programming, or energetic implants.

That's why energy coherence is about alignment to reclaim your original blueprint and recalibrate the energy centers to resonate with your true multi-dimensional identity.

The Spirit Body: Master Architecture of Multi-Dimensional Coherence

The terms "soul" and "spirit" are often used interchangeably. However, they actually refer to distinct aspects of your multi-dimensional identity. If the soul is the *experiencer* and the aspect of you navigating timelines, lives, and karmic sequences, then the Spirit Body is the *blueprint holder* and the original fractal of Source through which your entire multi-dimensional being unfolds.

It is not bound by time, and it does not evolve. It simply is a radiant intelligence, beyond form, and yet intimately woven through all layers of you.

The Spirit Body is the repository of your original Source codes, housing your full light architecture, your dimensional access, your creation templates, and your harmonic identity.

When people speak of connecting to "higher self," "inner truth," or "infinite intelligence," they are often touching into the edge of the Spirit Body, and without clear coherence, that signal can be distorted or misinterpreted. True access requires stability of frequency, energetic refinement,

Spirit vs. Soul: The Core Difference

Soul is personal. It remembers. It reincarnates. It gathers experience.

Spirit is transpersonal. It knows. It exists beyond karma or learning. It is the **direct extension of Source Consciousness**, carrying the core frequency pattern of your eternal Self.

and an activated vertical current through the Central Axis and extended chakra system.

Where Consciousness and Energy Meet

Composed of layers that exist well beyond the physical and emotional bodies, the Spirit Body is a defined energetic structure where consciousness and energy converge, occupying what could be considered pre-light or pre-sound states of reality.

The Spirit Body contains specific zones where:

- **Consciousness is stored** as geometric encoding and harmonic templates

- **Energy is directed** to guide incarnational sequences and physical experiences

- **Frequency is translated** into perceptual experience

These levels of organization can be described using the simplified concepts of Vital Light (the pure energetic substance of creation), Source Spark (the quantum spark or animating pulse from Source), and Spirit Matrix (the reservoir within the Spirit Body that holds the codes of consciousness and energy together in unity).

Together, these structures ensure that your being is more than reactive biology; it is a living interface between the eternal and the embodied.

To embody more of your Spirit Body is to live as a stabilized conduit of Source in form. This embodiment requires active cultivation of coherence across all layers of your multi-dimensional being:

- **Physical coherence** (cleansing toxicity and parasites, and strengthening the cellular matrix)

- **Emotional coherence** (purging trauma and distortion)

- **Energetic coherence** (clearing interference and density)

- **Mental coherence** (transcending linear thought and limiting narratives)

- **Dimensional coherence** (integrating higher stations of identity)

- **Spiritual coherence** (cultivating discernment, sovereignty, and authentic Source alignment)

When coherence is cultivated across these layers, the Spirit Body "descends" into form as the truest expression of you. You begin to feel the knowing before the thought, the direction before the decision, and the presence before the perception. You are no longer seeking Source because you are transmitting it.

Perhaps most importantly, the Spirit Body provides a shielding field of natural protection. When fully integrated, its harmonic frequency acts as a morphic boundary repelling lower-frequency interference, false signals, or energetic manipulation.

This is particularly vital for those engaging in multi-dimensional work, healing, or energetic facilitation. Without coherence in the Spirit Body, individuals may mistakenly channel external entities or misread energetic impressions. With coherence, you access truth directly from your eternal identity stream, free of distortion.

Stabilizing the Signal: Techniques for Strengthening Energy Coherence

Accessing Multi-Dimensional Intelligence is one thing. To hold it is another.

True spiritual evolution isn't about momentary peaks. It's about cultivating the capacity to remain coherent in high-frequency states, day after day, shift after shift. The Spirit Body cannot fully integrate if the lower bodies (mental, emotional, and physical) are full of static, density, or distortion. Coherence is what stabilizes the signal, allowing your multi-dimensional self to express through your incarnate form with clarity and precision.

Here are key practices and protocols to strengthen and sustain energetic coherence across all levels of your being:

1. Breath & Heart – Central Axis Synchronization (with 6-Pointed Scalar Breath)

Breathing multi-dimensionally from six spatial directions: front, back, left, right, above, and below. This is a scalar breathing technique designed to build vertical and horizontal pillar coherence.

Use the 6-Pointed Scalar Breath. Breathe in simultaneously from **all six directions—front, back, left, right, above, and below**. Envision your body at the center of a **star tetrahedron or 6-pointed cross**, drawing crystalline plasma light inward from the cosmic and elemental fields. As you inhale, feel the convergence of energy spiraling into your Central Axis center (located between the heart and throat). As you exhale, allow any discordant patterns, static, or density to be released back through the six directions, harmonized and neutralized.

Anchor awareness at the Central Axis point. This central node acts as the entry point for Source intelligence into the embodied form. Let your breath move through it like a still-point capacitor, syncing vertical flows (from Source above and Earth core below) with horizontal flows. This enhances both dimensional and spiritual coherence.

Infuse the breath with an emotion-tone. Layer the breath with a high harmonic frequency such as reverence, still-point love, or inner peace. These feeling-tones modulate your scalar wave signature and support the transduction of higher-dimensional instruction sets into your body.

2. Sound & Frequency Practices – Toning into the Central Axis

- Use **vocal toning.** Um-Ah-Um is a powerful and basic **trinity tone** used to initiate **still-point resonance** and begin scalar template activation.

  - Begin with the primal sound sequence: "UM–AH–UM." As you exhale, tone UM softly, allowing the vibration to resonate from your core and expand through the Central Axis point.
  - Focus the vibration through the Central Axis point. This point acts as a frequency hub, anchoring tones into the physical and pre-physical

template. As you tone, visualize the frequency rippling out in six directions (see 6-pointed breath field), linking with the Earth core and Cosmic Source simultaneously.

- Explore **432Hz and 528Hz** tones during meditation or rest to gently retune your field.

- Integrate **binaural beats** or **isochronic tones** for brainwave entrainment; especially useful during post-awakening instability to anchor delta, theta, or gamma wave coherence.

3. Movement as Energy Flow

- Practice **Qi Gong, Tai Chi, yoga or conscious movement** to circulate energy through the meridian and chakra systems.

- Use spiral-based motions to activate and align the central vertical current.

- Consider dancing, moving intuitively, or simply humming while moving. Remember, coherence isn't static, it flows.

4. Energetic Detox & Spiritual Hygiene: Clearing Density, Anchoring Discernment

True coherence requires clear space internally and externally. Detoxes are physical as well as emotional, mental, and vibrational. Every input, whether through food, media, EMFs, emotions, or symbols, can either enhance your coherence or fragment it.

- **Digital Detox & EMF Awareness**. Limit prolonged exposure to dissonant frequencies. Excess screen time, wireless interference, and digital chaos can fray the energetic field.

- **Environmental Detox**. Simplify your space. Remove objects, images, or symbols that carry stagnant or conflicting energy.

- **Energetic Baths**. Use magnesium-rich salts, structured water, or bicarbonate soaks with essential oils. These help dislodge energetic residues and calm the nervous system

Smell plays a powerful role in energetic cleansing. The olfactory system is directly connected to the limbic brain, the seat of memory and emotion. Sacred resins like frankincense, palo santo, copal, and sandalwood not only smell nice, they also trigger ancient memory, emotional release, and field purification. Use consciously, with intention. As the scent enters the body, imagine it *unlocking dormant codes*, releasing past emotional residue, and opening the breath.

5. The Geometry of Truth

The Lotus of Life and Source Spiral are based on base-12 scalar mathematics, the true language of eternal creation. These patterns mirror the natural flow of Source energy—breathing in, breathing out, expanding and returning, without distortion or energetic bleed.

Discernment is key.

When working with symbols, ask:

- Does this feel open or binding?
- Expansive or tight?
- Harmonizing or draining?

Your Spirit Body will always know, so let your coherence rather than your intellect guide your choice of sacred tools, images, and practices.

LOTUS OF LIFE

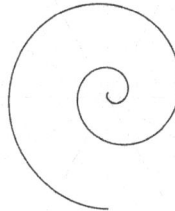

SOURCE SPIRAL

6. Energetic Sovereignty: Shielding, Centering, and Inner Authority

The more coherent you become, the more sensitive you become, not just to higher guidance, but to distortion, deception, and dissonance. This sensitivity is a gift and only when paired with sovereignty.

- Before engaging with teachings, tools, or beings, **pause at the Central Axis** and ask: *"Is this in alignment with my eternal Source expression?"*

- Speak boundaries. Declare sovereignty. And remember that your Spirit Body is your ultimate compass. No guru, guide, or grid can replace the knowing that rises from your coherence.

Living as a Coherent Field of Light

Energy coherence is more than a state. It is a signature. A resonance. A declaration to the universe that you are willing to stabilize the infinite within the finite, and that you can hold Source light without distortion.

To walk coherently in a multi-dimensional world is to become a living temple where sound, light, and memory move as one. It is to activate the Central Axis and allow the Spirit Body to descend through you as sustained presence.

Your breath becomes a bridge. Your voice becomes a tuning fork. Your choices become code. You begin to recognize where frequencies are inverted, where symbols deceive, where energy is siphoned instead of regenerated. You no longer mistake false light for truth. Coherence breeds discernment, and discernment births sovereignty.

This is the return of true Multi-Dimensional Intelligence in action.

In the next chapter, you'll step deeper into this potential. You'll discover how coherence empowers you to bend time, shift timelines, and create reality through precise, embodied alignment with your Spirit Body, your Source field, and your multi-dimensional blueprint. When your energy is coherent, your intent becomes command. Your presence becomes creation. And the field responds.

INTEGRATION KEYS
Energy Coherence: The Engine of Embodied Multi-Dimensionality

- Energy coherence stabilizes the multi-dimensional self, allowing you to hold multiple layers of awareness without fragmentation, confusion, or energetic collapse.

- Your state of coherence is measurable in the body, mind, and field. Breath, posture, attention, and emotion all influence your internal alignment. When coherence is present, information flows freely between the seen and unseen dimensions.

- Multi-Dimensional Intelligence provides a foundation for maintaining clarity in complex environments. Coherence acts as a tuning mechanism, sharpening perception, regulating nervous system activity, and strengthening your field as a transmitter of precise frequency.

- When you embody coherence, you no longer react to chaos; you become a harmonizing force. Your presence communicates order, your choices carry resonance, and your signal becomes a stabilizing architecture in the collective field.

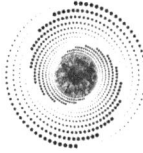

Chapter Seven

Timeline Navigation: Quantum Reality Creation

Introduction
The Illusion of a Fixed Reality

Do you remember the movie *Back to the Future*? Marty McFly accidentally travels 30 years into the past, tweaks a few key events, and returns to a present that's very different. His family's dynamic has shifted, and his entire timeline has been altered by one pivotal moment. While it is entertaining sci-fi, this movie also hints at a deeper truth.

What if your past isn't fixed, your future isn't predetermined, and this present moment is just one frequency in a sea of infinite now-points?

You are conditioned to live by clocks and calendars, aligning your life to the illusion of a straight linear progression with your past behind you and the future ahead. Yet time is not a line; it is a lens, and one that can distort or reveal reality depending on the frequency of your consciousness. You are not simply traveling through time; rather time is moving through you, shaped by your state of awareness.

I recall a time walking in nature and being so deeply immersed in the moment, so completely present, that I suddenly realized hours had passed, even though it felt like minutes. Days later, I had a dream so vivid that it lingered for weeks. Then, while visiting a new city I'd never been to, I turned a corner and froze. Everything was familiar; the café, the sound of the street musician, even the couple laughing on the bench. It was exactly as I'd seen it in my dream. A deep déjà vu awareness rippled through me, as if I had arrived at a point in time I had already lived... except in another timeline.

Experiences such as these nudge at the edges of understanding. They are a reminder that time may not be as linear or as stable as you may have been taught and led to believe.

Welcome to the quantum reality playground, where science, mysticism, and consciousness converge. In this space, time is elastic. Space is optional. And your decisions shape the future, split it, multiply it, and ripple through realities you may not be consciously aware of. Timelines are not sequential here; they're simultaneous.

You can be a passive traveler through time, or the navigator, the architect, and the tuner of timelines.

This chapter invites you to throw out the outdated GPS of linear causality and activate your quantum compass. Rather than managing time, you're mastering it. You'll explore the science of superposition, the subtle art of quantum jumping, and the hidden forces attempting to steer mass consciousness down certain timelines. More importantly, you'll learn how to recognize these timeline patterns and intentionally shift into sovereign, high-frequency versions of reality aligned with your multi-dimensional self.

"When I stand at a potent site, a place rich with energy or history, the dimensional shift becomes accessible. I may find myself not in today's Thursday, but in a Thursday thousands of years ago. My gift as a Sacred Site Whisperer lets me 'tune' into the strongest signal present. Sometimes I land in an unintended timeline and must scan again with focused consciousness to find a deeper or older layer. The metaphor I use is a radio wave. Dozens of signals are in the air. If you know how, you can tune in."

–John Paul Eagleheart, Shaman & Sacred Site Whisperer

This is real-world alchemy and *waking up inside the future you've already chosen.*

KEY QUESTIONS FOR EXPLORING IN CHAPTER SEVEN

◊   What if the version of you living your highest potential already exists?

◊   How many of your current beliefs are shaping the timeline you're in?

◊   What signal are you sending to stabilize the reality you step into next?

Reality Glitches, Speed Hacks, and the Time-Bending Game We're In

Picture a ceiling fan spinning so rapidly that it appears motionless, reduced to a blur, an illusion of stillness. Or recall the film *Lucy*, where the protagonist absorbs immense knowledge and energy, causing time to freeze, reverse, and dissolve altogether. These moments are more than a cinematic spectacle. They reveal a deeper truth: when perception accelerates or slows down, reality begins to shift.

Time and space, long assumed to be the stable foundations of reality, begin to dissolve under close observation, and even more so through acceleration. If this reality is a game, then time is one of its central rule sets, and like all rules, it can be hacked.

Time is one of the greatest mysteries of existence, yet it is often perceived as a fixed, linear path with the past leading to the present, and present leading to future. However, modern physics suggests a very different reality. First, time and space are inseparable; one cannot exist without the other. After all, it takes time to move from one space to another, and that very act of movement alters your experience of time.

In *Back to the Future*, Marty McFly travels back in time and accidentally interferes with the first meeting between his parents, jeopardizing his own existence. This scenario illustrates one of the most well-known time travel conundrums: the Grandfather Paradox. The paradox poses the question: *What if you traveled back in time and prevented your grandfather from meeting your grandmother?* If you succeeded, you would never be born; yet if you were never born, how could you have gone back in time in the first place? This creates a logical loop that highlights the fragility of a single, linear timeline, where past, present, and future are tightly interwoven and causality must remain intact.

Albert Einstein's Theory of Relativity disrupted our traditional sense of time, showing it to be a flexible dimension influenced by the movement of objects and observers through space, as well as by gravity. When an object or the observer themselves moves at high velocity or is near a massive body, time for them slows down relative to someone farther away or moving more slowly. This suggests that time is not fixed, but relative. Still, this theory operates largely within the boundaries of a single continuum.

Quantum mechanics, however, offers an even stranger possibility, and one that elegantly sidesteps the Grandfather Paradox altogether. According to the Many-Worlds Interpretation, every quantum event, every decision, every possibility results in the branching of the universe into parallel timelines. In this view, if Marty prevented his parents from meeting, he wouldn't vanish from existence—he would simply transition into a parallel timeline where he was never born, while the original version of reality would continue on elsewhere. Nothing is erased; it simply diverges.

This idea has long fascinated philosophers, physicists, and storytellers alike. Philip K. Dick, one of science fiction's most prophetic voices, built his body of work around the uncertainty of reality and the multiplicity of timelines. In *The Man in the High Castle*, he imagines a world where the Axis powers won World War II—a parallel history coexisting beside our own. In *Ubik*, characters struggle to discern which version of reality is "real" as they shift through layers of time and perception. Dick's narratives often explored the unsettling notion that our sense of identity, memory, and time itself may be far less stable than we believe.

This fascination continues in modern cinema. Films like *Interstellar*, *The Matrix*, and *Everything Everywhere All at Once* probe the nature of parallel timelines, nonlinear perception, and reality's malleability. These stories speak to an intuitive understanding—perhaps even a buried memory—that you are not bound to one fixed timeline. That there are versions of you who made different choices, and that it may be possible, consciously or unconsciously, to shift between them.

In *Interstellar*, time is revealed to be malleable, influenced by gravity and perception. The protagonist, Cooper, experiences time dilation near a massive black hole.

Cooper's journey into the black hole, Gargantua, culminates in an extraordinary moment of transition. Instead of being crushed by gravitational forces, he finds himself within a tesseract, a four-dimensional construct that allows him to navigate time as a spatial dimension. This pivotal scene offers a profound metaphor for quantum timeline navigation.

In physics, a black hole represents a point of infinite gravitational pull where the known laws of space and time break down. It collapses three-dimensional space into a singularity, effectively dissolving the linear flow of time as is commonly understood. Entering a black hole is symbolic of entering the zero-point field, the still-point of all potential, where time, space, and identity become fluid.

The tesseract, a higher-dimensional hypercube, allows Cooper to perceive time not as a linear progression but as a landscape. He can move through past moments, select different frequency "coordinates," and interact with reality across time, which is similar to what occurs during deep states of consciousness or non-local perception.

This moment in the film brilliantly illustrates what physicist David Bohm and other pioneers of quantum consciousness suggest: that space and time are projected dimensions from a deeper, unified field. This notion aligns with the idea of consciousness stepping beyond the boundaries of the local space-time vector into the Unified Morphogenetic Field; a grid-like holographic structure where all possible timelines coexist and can be accessed via frequency and intention.

Cooper, in essence, becomes the observer collapsing the wave function. Through love for his daughter, an energetic signature of coherence, he sends a signal across time. This mirrors the idea that consciousness itself is the architect of timelines. Just as Cooper reaches his daughter through the tesseract, you too can reach across time through elevated states of awareness, deep resonance, and intentional alignment.

What *Interstellar* dramatizes is the very real, though often unseen, capacity of human consciousness to operate beyond the constraints of 3D time and space. It is a cinematic glimpse into the mechanics of Multi-Dimensional Intelligence and quantum creation.

The Matrix explores the notion that reality is not what it seems, and that multiple layers of perception exist. The moment Neo takes the red pill, he awakens to an entirely new paradigm, shifting into a different "timeline" of awareness. The film suggests that your beliefs and perceptions determine which reality you experience, a concept that resonates with quantum theory and the role of the observer in shaping outcomes.

In the award-winning movie, *Everything Everywhere All at Once*, the protagonist navigates a multiverse of possibilities, encountering different versions of herself based on the choices she made, or did not make. The film highlights the idea that all possibilities exist simultaneously and that consciousness can jump between them. This mirrors the concept of quantum jumping; by aligning with a different version of yourself, one that has already achieved a goal or mastered a skill, you can shift your trajectory toward that timeline.

Traditional views of time compare it to a river flowing in one direction from past to future. However, a more accurate metaphor is an ocean with waves (timelines) moving in all directions, overlapping and shifting based on your perception. Imagine being in the middle of a vast ocean. The waves around you represent all possible timelines. Some waves rise and rush toward you, others collapse and recede, and some swirl in unexpected patterns. You can choose to ride a specific wave, alter its course, or step back and let another one approach. This is how you navigate reality, whether consciously or unconsciously, selecting which timeline to step into.

Sometimes the smallest decisions have the greatest impact. Perhaps you can recall a moment when you hesitated before making a choice; something as simple as turning left instead of right. Yet, at that moment, your choice altered the course of your life. Had you gone the other way, perhaps you would not have met a person who played a significant role in your journey. These subtle shifts are a reminder that your decisions constantly shape reality.

The Science of Timelines and Quantum Realities

In the quantum world, reality is not a fixed thing; it's a probability cloud. Particles exist in multiple states simultaneously until observed; a phenomenon known as superposition.

Erwin Schrödinger illustrated this through his now-famous thought experiment: Schrödinger's Cat. In summary, a cat is placed in a sealed box with a vial of poison triggered to open and poison the cat. Until someone opens the box, the cat exists in a bizarre quantum limbo, both alive and dead at the same time. It's only when the observer looks inside that one version becomes "real" and the other vanishes from conscious perception.

But what if it doesn't vanish?

What if that other version, the one where the cat lives or dies differently, continues to unfold in a parallel timeline, still real, yet just out of sync with your current frequency of awareness?

This is where it gets personal.

If particles and, therefore, reality, exist in multiple states, then so do you. You are not a single, fixed identity but a constellation of possible selves. Multiple versions of you exist in potential: the one who said yes to the relationship and built a life around it, and the one who walked away and reclaimed their independence. The version of you who took the job offer overseas and now lives immersed in another culture, and the one who stayed in your hometown, weaving deeper roots. There's a you who became a parent, and a you who chose freedom over family. A you who followed your artistic calling despite the risks, and another who chose security and a steady paycheck. Every decision is a pivot point in the quantum field, and each choice generates a ripple across timelines, where alternate versions of your life continue to play out in parallel realities. These are quantum realities. And when you tune your awareness, you may feel echoes of these other selves nudging you, guiding you, reminding you of paths taken or not.

Superposition isn't just a strange quirk of quantum physics, it's the blueprint of your lived experience. In quantum mechanics, superposition describes the ability of a system to exist in multiple states at once. Schrödinger's Cat, both dead and alive, is a model for how your probable choices are suspended in potentiality until a decision is made. Blake Crouch's *Dark Matter* dives deeply into this idea. In both the novel and the Apple TV series, a consciousness-altering device, a literal box, allows the protagonist to access alternate timelines, each of them an expression of a different life choice. He imagines possibilities, and he walks through them. Similarly, *Constellation* on Apple TV explores what happens when timelines collide or fracture when you become aware of other versions of reality and begin to question which one is truly yours. These aren't just science fiction plots. They're dramatizations of quantum truths. Superposition is your natural state before the wave collapses, before you decide who you are and what you want to experience. Multi-Dimensional Intelligence is your capacity to sense these parallel tracks and consciously align with the one that holds your highest resonance.

Every decision you make collapses one potential into your lived experience, but the others don't disappear. They fork off, like branches from a tree, forming an intricate web of coexisting timelines. The version you didn't choose still exists; it's just in another stream of probability, navigated by a different "you" — a probable self.

The Double-Slit Experiment, which involves observing firing particles at a wall with two slits, echoes this strange quantum behavior. When unobserved, they behave like waves passing through both slits at once and creating an interference pattern, as if reality is still fluid. However, the moment you place a device to watch, the particles "decide" to go through just one slit, collapsing into a single outcome. Observation changes behavior, while awareness stabilizes the field.

This suggests something astonishing:

- While you are experiencing reality, you are also selecting it.

- Your focus is the cursor and your belief is the click.

- Where attention goes, reality grows.

Reality is like a vast jukebox of infinite songs where every timeline is a different melody. All are playing simultaneously, and you only hear the track your consciousness is tuned to. When you shift your frequency, which includes your emotions, thoughts, and expectations, you change the track. That's how timeline navigation works.

And the music you didn't select? It's still playing... just not through your speaker.

The more intentionally you observe and engage with a particular outcome, the more that outcome stabilizes into your reality. The universe does not ask what's objectively true. It reflects back what you believe is true and what you emotionally accept as possible.

Imagine you're holding a remote control. Every button is a version of your life. Most people are stuck watching the same channel, not realizing they can change it. However, you've just remembered the remote is in your hand, so ask yourself, *"What timeline am I tuned into right now?"* Without judgment, notice the "channel" and the emotional tone, the narrative running through your mind, the themes unfolding in your life. Now ask, *"What channel do I want to be on instead?"*

You are the observer, the tuner, and the timeline stabilizer. The other versions of you are still out there, running parallel, waiting for your consciousness to catch up.

Parallel You: Meeting the Self Who Made a Different Choice

Have you ever walked into a room and felt an uncanny sense of familiarity, even though you've never been there before? Or woken from a dream so vivid that the waking world feels like an illusion? That tingle or that whisper in your consciousness could be more than coincidence. It may be a bleed-through from a parallel version of you: a glimpse into a timeline where you chose the unknown over the familiar.

You are living through what some describe as a Chaotic Node, a cosmic convergence point where multiple timelines intersect, blur, and occasionally collapse. It's as if the multiverse is remixing itself. During these phases, the veil thins. Time becomes fluid. Identity becomes quantum.

Every decision you've ever made, or didn't make, has created a probable self. These selves are not fictional. They are active timelines playing out in the background of the quantum field. Your consciousness can tune into them; it's like selecting a different version of a video game character, already upgraded and leveled up.

This phenomenon is demonstrated in cultural anomalies called The Mandela Effect. For example, millions of people vividly remember Nelson Mandela dying in prison in the 1980s, even though history shows he was released and went on to become president of South Africa. Other timeline glitches include people recalling the name "Berenstein" in the Berenstain Bear series, as spelled with an "e." Or Mr. Monopoly, the mascot of the board game, wearing a monocle. These are not just memory errors; they may be glimpses into nearby timelines once occupied or still occupied in another strand of reality. Bring to mind a grand, infinite library where each book on the shelf is

Cynthia Sue Larson, author of *Quantum Jumps*, writes: *"At every moment, we stand at the crossroads of all possible futures. Quantum jumping is the act of aligning with the version of yourself who's already living your desired outcome—and bringing that version into your now."*

a version of you, a probable self who made different choices, lived different lives, and followed different desires. You can pull down any book at any moment. You can read the story, and you can merge with it.

The version of you who didn't move abroad, who stayed in the relationship, who took the leap or didn't, all continue to unfold, encoded within the quantum field. Some of these versions may evolve into higher expressions of mastery, and others may spiral into stagnation or fear. However, all of them offer insight.

And the most powerful shift of all? The recognition that you can access them. You can become them.

You are not a single timeline-bound being; you are a multi-dimensional explorer with full access to the selves you've been, are becoming, and could still become. And when you align with a probable self who has already mastered what you're reaching for, you step into their world.

So yes, there are many versions of you, including the idealized versions who "got it right," as well as the you who struggled, failed, played small, or danced in the shadows. You are the brave, the broken, the brilliant, the betrayer, the beloved. All of it. All of you.

In this polarized game of reality, you get to explore the contrast between good and bad, light and dark, rich and poor, not as punishment, but as play. You've chosen to dive into all realms of expression so you can remember yourself through experience. And while one version of you is chasing the light, another may be navigating the dark. Both are valid. Both are divine.

You are not one self, you are *many*.
You are not trapped, you are *travelling*.

Dreamtime, Lucid Realities, and The Quantum Internet of Consciousness

Dreams are often described as the brain's way of processing unconscious fragments. But they may also be something more, such as gateways into parallel timelines, glimpses of realities you temporarily inhabit.

Anyone who's ever awakened from a dream sweating, weeping, exhilarated, or exhausted knows: some dreams feel more real than waking life. Perhaps that's because they are. Perhaps your consciousness is time-traveling through the quantum field, experiencing alternate lives, jumping timelines, or reconnecting with your multi-dimensional selves while your body sleeps. Lucid dreaming gives you an opportunity to explore them.

Lucid dreaming is the art of becoming awake and aware within a dream. In lucid dreams, you realize that you're dreaming and have the ability to influence the environment, the characters, and the outcomes. You can slay the dragon, fly through cities, or rewrite your story. And more than simply entertainment, it's training you for conscious reality creation.

Enter the Aboriginal Dreamtime

For many Aboriginal people, time does not flow in a straight line. Their concept of Dreamtime, or The Dreaming, is a vast multi-dimensional reality where past, present, and future co-exist. Unlike Western perspectives that treat time as a sequence of events, the Aboriginal worldview sees time as something woven together, fluid, nonlinear, and accessible through higher states of awareness.

Dreamtime is both the creation epoch and an ongoing living force that connects people to their ancestors, the land, and cosmic consciousness. Aboriginal elders, known as *Lore Keepers*, serve as custodians of this knowledge and possess an extraordinary ability to access other realms. Some accounts describe their remarkable capacity to traverse vast distances in the physical world through what appears to be teleportation or bilocation, suggesting an advanced understanding of reality beyond conventional physics.

In many ways, the Aboriginal people exemplify Multi-Dimensional Intelligence through their ability to exist in and navigate multiple layers of reality at once. Their practices of songlines, sacred storytelling, and ritual dream-walking demonstrate their innate mastery of shifting between states of consciousness and interacting with parallel timelines.

Dreamtime operates like a quantum internet; nonlinear, holographic, and endlessly accessible. Just as every computer connected to the web can access the whole, you can, through focused intention and inner stillness, access the living library of timelines encoded within the field.

This is Multi-Dimensional Intelligence in practice:

» Dreamwalking as timeline navigation
» Songlines as vibrational passwords

» Memory as location

» Consciousness as the bridge

Some Aboriginal mystics enter a state called Deep Dreaming, where they receive messages, rewrite the past, and tune into alternative futures. This aligns with lucid dreaming, quantum jumping, and the ability to consciously direct reality shifts.

Rather than seeing dreams as fantasy, the Aboriginal way and the quantum way invite you to honor them as realities. Doorways. Missions. And sometimes, as warnings or initiations.

By tuning into this ancient understanding, you no longer passively drift through sleep, because you become dreamtime navigators capable of retrieving wisdom, healing the past, and scripting new timelines before waking.

For those seeking to become more intentional in navigating their own timelines, these Aboriginal practices provide profound inspiration. Rather than seeing reality as something fixed and rigid, they invite you to perceive it as an ongoing dance between energy, consciousness, and creation.

Timeline Navigation: Conscious vs. Unconscious Shifting

Reality can be thought of as a *Choose-Your-Own-Adventure Book*, with each moment presenting a decision that alters the storyline. By becoming aware of these choices, you can rewrite the narrative and step into a desired reality.

Incorporating the wisdom of Aboriginal traditions, you can use visualization techniques like songlines, imagining a different path within a landscape where every step is encoded with intention. This merges physical movement with energetic alignment, reinforcing the desired timeline shift.

Reality Rewind Exercise: A powerful practice for shifting timelines...

• Recall a past moment where a different decision could have been made.

• Mentally 'rewind' time and visualize making a new choice.

• Observe how this shifts your current emotional and energetic state.

The Aboriginal Dreamtime teaches that timelines are alive, adaptable, and accessible through awareness. Just as an elder can enter Dreamtime to communicate with ancestors, you too can consciously engage with different versions of yourself and the probabilities unfolding around you.

As the Dreamtime reveals a multi-dimensional map of existence, so do your thoughts, emotions, and inner frequencies act as a compass, guiding which timelines you activate. Whether you are asleep or awake, you're tuning your field. You are always emitting and broadcasting a signal.

And the universe responds to your frequency.

Quantum Reality Creation: Shaping Your Future

In this game of timelines, you attract what you are. Your frequency is your signature and energetic identity card. Every timeline and potential version of your life has a frequency tag attached to it.

This is the essence of resonance.

If you're humming a note in a room full of tuning forks, only the fork vibrating at the same frequency as your voice will begin to sing with you. That's resonance. And that's how reality works. Every belief you hold, every emotion you embody, sends out a vibrational pulse. And the timelines that match that pulse start singing back.

So, if you want to live in a timeline of health, ease, or abundance, rather than chase it, you become it. You match the rhythm and embody the song.

How to Measure Your Frequency

You don't need a mystical device to check your frequency, because your reality is already doing that for you. But there are tools, both scientific and esoteric, that attempt to map internal states of consciousness and coherence.

Here are a few reference points:

- **Heart Rate Variability (HRV):** A marker of adaptability and emotional regulation. Higher HRV = higher coherence.

- **Brainwave States:** Gamma waves (30–100 Hz) are associated with expanded perception and integration.

- **Emotional Barometer:** Love, peace, joy = expansive. Fear, guilt, shame = contractive.

- **Muscle Testing / Biofeedback:** These offer insight into energetic alignment and dissonance.

- **Synchronicity & Flow:** When your internal state is clear and resonant, life feels effortless. Doors open, ideas flow, and you feel "on track."

One of the most widely referenced tools in consciousness work is David R. Hawkins' *Map of Consciousness,* which calibrates emotional and spiritual states on a logarithmic scale from 0 to 1000 using applied kinesiology. According to this map, shame vibrates at 20, guilt at 30, courage at 200, and enlightenment at 700+.

It's an elegant model and one that has offered structure and guidance to many on their spiritual journey.

But here's a worthy inquiry: Who created the scale? Who calibrated it? And through what filters?

The entire system is based on Hawkins' own muscle testing experiments and subjective interpretation. While powerful, it is still just a lens and belief-generated construct filtered through one man's consciousness, cultural context, and metaphysical model. This doesn't make it invalid. It simply means discernment is always required.

The deeper message is that your own frequency, your lived experience, and your intuition are as valid as any external system, regardless of how revered it is.

The Role of Sound and Light Waves in Reality Creation

After exploring resonance and the internal mechanics of frequency alignment, it is time to go into the architecture of creation itself.

First of all, creation does not begin with matter, but with sound. It is sound that gives rise to light, and light that gives rise to form. These are not metaphorical concepts, but energetic structures embedded into the core fabric of the multi-dimensional universe.

Before there was light, there was sound as scalar standing waves, which are non-linear, non-physical patterns of intention. These sound fields form pre-light blueprints from which light fields emerge as flashes of scalar radiation.

Every "thing" in the perceived universe, including you, is built upon these sound-light grids—an eternal harmonic architecture. From this matrix, flash line sequences emerge, orchestrating the continual pulsing of energy units into manifestation and back out again. This happens at such an incomprehensible speed that reality appears solid and continuous; similar to how a movie appears to be smooth and seamless when it's actually a rapid sequence of frames.

Reality as Flash Line Sequences

What you perceive as solid matter is simply energy structured through rhythmic pulses of light and sound. In truth, your reality is flashing on and off in rapid succession, micro-moments of materialization and dematerialization. This "flicker-rate" is governed by the scalar templates beneath your DNA and consciousness.

Reality is not solid or fixed; you are riding a strobe-light of existence. And here's the incredible part: In the brief micro-gap between the flashes, all quantum probabilities exist. This is the zero-point moment and the creation code waiting for your directive.

The Zero-Point Field is a domain of infinite potential energy, undifferentiated and still. It is the field described by quantum physics and mystics alike where:

Time and space are illusions

Thought, intention, and frequency generate reality

Consciousness precedes matter

The zero-point field is the true singularity and a field of total creative possibility. To enter it is to step outside the matrix of time and space and into the creator field itself. This is where timeline shifts occur by frequency match.

If you can influence your state of awareness during this "off" phase, when reality de-coheres, you can determine which timeline, which frame, which potential becomes your next embodied experience.

In other words, manifestation doesn't happen in the flash. It happens in the pause.

Think of reality as a filmstrip with each "now" moment as a frame. Your consciousness is the projector, choosing which frame to light up. Unlike a standard projector, this one allows you to insert new frames, rewrite scenes, or even switch movie reels mid-play if you learn to access the pause between flashes.

The Symphony of Creation

Just as a tuning fork activates another tuning fork vibrating

Quantum Jumping Exercise: Aligning with Your Desired Reality

If all potential timelines already exist encoded in the morphogenetic field, then your work is to tune into the version of you who already lives there.

Try this guided process:

1. Identify the Future You

Imagine a version of you who has already achieved your goal See them. Feel them. Sense how they walk, speak, breathe.

2. Align Your Frequency

Ask yourself:

- What does this version of me believe that I don't yet?
- What emotional state do they embody?
- What habits and boundaries do they maintain?
- Begin integrating these now.

3. Step into the Timeline

Visualize stepping into their body.

Let their energy become your own.

Say: *"I merge with this self now."*

4. Live As If You've Already Jumped

Make micro-decisions today that affirm this shift.

Speak, dress, and move as if that version is already real, because in the field, it is.

with the same frequency, your intentions act as sound tones rippling through the field. When you emit the resonance of your chosen reality, the universe responds by mirroring your energetic command.

This universe is a living template of morphogenetic instruction sets and you are the conductor.

Collective Consciousness, Mass Influence, and Timeline Shifts

Having explored how you shape reality through the oscillation of sound, light, and intention, underpinned by scalar architecture and flash line sequences, it's time to zoom out, because you're not manifesting in isolation.

As your personal field emits a frequency that magnetizes timelines, the collective consciousness of humanity functions as a planetary resonance field, generating large-scale shared experiences. Societies, movements, innovations, even disasters, emerge from the harmonic convergence of mass belief structures.

This shared field, when coherent, births new realities. However, when it is manipulated, it can trap billions into timelines not of their conscious choosing.

The question becomes: **Are you dreaming your future into being… or being dreamed into someone else's design?**

Collective belief systems are active creators of shared timelines. Consider the world before the Wright brothers achieved flight. A mass belief system cracked open when their machine lifted off. A shift in possibility. A portal into a new timeline. Once believed impossible, flight became ordinary. So too, with the invention of electricity, space travel, the internet—all of which were ridiculed until they became the norm.

While belief systems may evolve organically, they are also engineered. Humanity may not be navigating a purely natural ascension of consciousness; instead, it may be subtly steering itself through pre-programmed collective loops. This means that, in some cases, rather than expanding in infinite directions, the multiverse is being narrowed by design.

Many believe we are living through a timeline bifurcation, a moment where realities are splitting based on vibrational alignments and mass decision points. A collective crossroads where one script ends and another begins.

The Tavistock Institute and the Engineering of Reality

One of the most significant yet hidden influences on human consciousness has been social engineering organizations such as The Tavistock Institute of Human Relations. Founded in the UK in 1947, Tavistock has played a pivotal role in shaping mass psychology, propaganda, and perception management. Originally established to study psychological warfare, Tavistock pioneered mass mind control techniques that have been used in government, media, education, and corporate structures worldwide.

Tavistock's methods are based on herd psychology and social conditioning, with the idea that individuals conform to collective thought patterns, often without realizing it. Through media manipulation, crisis orchestration, and predictive programming, Tavistock has influenced global consciousness, subtly guiding public opinion and behavior.

Examples of Collective Reality Manipulation:

1. Media Influence & Perception Management

   o The manufacturing of consent through media narratives (e.g., framing certain global events as inevitable, reinforcing fear-based responses).

   o Repetitive messaging designed to normalize previously unthinkable ideas (e.g., gradual acceptance of mass surveillance, loss of personal freedoms, digital currency control).

   o Through the entertainment industry's predictive programming, where movies and TV shows foreshadow real-world events, conditioning the public to accept them as natural occurrences (e.g., *Black Mirror* series influencing tech adoption, *The Simpsons* show predicting future events)

2. False Flags & Crisis Engineering

   o Wars and major political shifts often follow a pattern of problem-reaction-solution; a crisis is fabricated to justify increased societal control or intervention.

o Public emotions are manipulated through staged fear-based events, ensuring that people react instead of consciously choosing their own response.

3. Herd Mentality & Social Compliance

o The Asch Conformity Experiment showed that individuals will knowingly choose an incorrect answer in a group setting simply to conform.

o The Milgram Experiment demonstrated how authority figures can coerce people into actions against their moral judgment, showing the power of compliance programming.

o Mass social movements are often orchestrated rather than organic, using astroturfing techniques (fake grassroots efforts) to manipulate public perception and enforce collective conformity.

4. Hijacking Spiritual Movements

o The New Age movement has been infiltrated by disinformation designed to pacify rather than empower. The idea that "everything is love and light" can discourage critical thinking and discernment, making individuals more susceptible to external control.

o The emphasis on external saviors, galactic federations, or channeled entities shifts focus away from personal sovereignty and direct consciousness mastery.

Expanding Consciousness Beyond the Control Grid

If mass belief systems are engineered, how do you break free and reclaim your ability to navigate timelines with conscious intention? This is where Multi-Dimensional Intelligence becomes a critical tool which allows you to:

• Develop your discernment to recognize programming and manipulation.

• Expand your perception beyond conditioned belief structures.

• Detach from mass fear narratives and reclaim sovereignty over your consciousness.

- Activate timeline awareness to shift out of manipulated realities and into self-directed experiences.

A key to breaking free from the control matrix is learning to recognize frequency manipulation. Every emotion and thought emits a frequency. When mass consciousness is programmed into fear, division, and scarcity, it keeps individuals locked in lower timelines, unable to access higher awareness and alternative possibilities. By shifting personal resonance, one can break the cycle and step into a reality governed by clarity, sovereignty, and conscious creation.

Conscious Timeline Shifting: Choosing Your Reality

If belief systems shape reality, then reclaiming your sovereignty begins with choosing which beliefs and which frequencies you wish to broadcast. Every moment is a timeline portal. Every thought, emotion, and decision tunes your field to a new potential.

How to Discern Timeline Manipulation

- Does an event create an immediate, emotionally charged reaction? (If yes, it may be designed to trigger mass consciousness into alignment with a specific agenda.)

- Are you adopting a belief because it was repeatedly reinforced, or because you have deeply examined it yourself?

- Are you reacting out of fear or personal empowerment? Fear-based reactions tend to lock people into pre-designed narratives.

- Does the reality you are being presented with feel restrictive or expansive? True awakening expands perception, whereas manipulation creates rigid mental constructs.

This is where Multi-Dimensional Intelligence becomes your compass, and with it, you move from being a passenger on someone else's track to becoming the conductor of your own multi-dimensional reality.

Below is a guide to shifting from unconscious programming into conscious reality design.

How to Reclaim Your Sovereignty & Shift into Higher Timelines

1. Awaken Inner Awareness

- Develop practices of stillness and presence that dissolve distortion.
- Begin to discern: Is this thought mine? Or is it a broadcast I've absorbed?

2. Unplug from Artificial Constructs

- Limit exposure to media and narratives engineered to polarize or diminish
- Engage in mental fasting by stepping away from noise to reconnect with knowing.

3. Master Your Frequency

- Shift from reaction to resonance; from reactivity to intentional emotion.
- Use sound (toning, music), breath, and movement to recalibrate your field.

4. Create Consciously, Live Intentionally

- Speak your reality into being as if it has already happened.
- Use quantum techniques like timeline jumping, future writing, and identity embodiment
- Make choices from the timeline you wish to inhabit, not the one you wish to leave.

The Timeline Console

Picture yourself sitting in front of a master control panel where each dial adjusts a frequency, emotion, belief, action, and memory, and each lever shifts a trajectory. The screen before you shows infinite versions of Earth, of your life, of yourself, and you can choose which one to step into today.

Yes, collective consciousness is being influenced, and yes, belief systems are often engineered, but now you've been shown the interface, the command line and the underlying code of creation.

The more you cultivate Multi-Dimensional Intelligence, the less susceptible you are to programmed timelines, and the more capable you become of writing your own.

Current scientific models struggle to account for the bulk of the universe. Dark matter and dark energy, which comprise over 95% of all that exists, remain enigmatic. Entanglement defies space-time logic. Memory, intuition, and the mechanism of consciousness remain unsolved. Olav Drageset, a physicist and systems theorist exploring the intersection of consciousness and cosmology,

Becoming a Timeline Master

Reality is like playing chess: Each move you make opens new potential outcomes.

Future Memory Technique: Write out your ideal reality as if it has already happened.

Reality Audit: Identify thoughts, emotions, and beliefs shaping your timeline.

describes this as the "science gap," a territory where subjective and objective realities begin to merge. The Multi-Dimensional Intelligence framework navigates this gap, suggesting that your choices, awareness, and resonance shape the probabilities you live in. In this light, timeline navigation becomes less about cause-and-effect and more about coherence with unseen fields.

Like Cooper in *Interstellar*, you too are navigating through the gravitational pull of memories, emotions, and beliefs. You are standing at the edge of the black hole, being invited into your own singularity. The moment you drop the illusion of linear time, you enter the tesseract of consciousness. Remember:

- **Your heart is the gravitational transmitter** broadcasting intentions beyond time.

- **Your DNA is the multi-dimensional compass** resonating with certain timelines over others.

- **Your Multi-Dimensional Intelligence is the bridge**, the wormhole, the navigational intelligence that allows you to align with the future that already exists in potential.

INTEGRATION KEYS
Timeline Navigation and Quantum Reality Creation

- Reality is sculpted by frequency, attention, and alignment. Through Multi-Dimensional Intelligence, you gain the ability to sense timelines as living structures, each carrying different outcomes, lessons, and resonance.

- Timeline navigation begins with attunement. As you refine your awareness, you feel the subtle tugs of possible selves and parallel paths. Multi-Dimensional Intelligence enables you to track these options without overwhelm and choose with precision.

- Every decision generates momentum. The more aligned your internal field, the more rapidly external shifts take shape. You begin to witness the collapse of obsolete patterns and the emergence of quantum opportunities.

- Multi-Dimensional Intelligence reveals your role as a conscious reality architect, someone who doesn't chase destiny but shapes it by holding a steady signal and responding from the deepest layers of knowing.

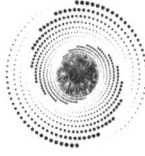

Radiant Architecture: Living as a Multi-Dimensional Human

Introduction

Threshold Activation: The Dissolution of the Simulated Self

Perhaps you've spent a lifetime constructing an identity out of memory, trauma, stories, and systems. Now, everything that once defined you, such as your name, nationality, gender, goals, is being revealed as scaffolding for something vaster— a multi-dimensional field of consciousness that was never meant to be managed by the mind, but rather to be embodied through your frequency.

The intention of this chapter is to shatter and collapse the idea that you're here to ascend and evolve to something expansive.

You've traveled far through the landscapes of consciousness into time loops, light codes, and fields of memory that exist beyond form. Along the way, you've touched frequencies that once felt distant and abstract, only to discover they've always been within reach.

You have now reached a crossing point. From here, you will move from concept into current. From understanding into transmission. From sensing potential to living as it.

Multi-Dimensional Intelligence is not reserved for altered states or quiet meditation. It is a living current woven into how you make decisions, how you speak, how you hold yourself in the field of life. It shapes your relationships, your creativity, your leadership ability, and your capacity to move through space as an aligned expression of Source.

Your journey may have included rituals, mentors, sacred teachings, and profound breakthroughs. Each of them opened a door. Yet there comes a moment when the external path fades and the codes begin to rise from within. Real guidance no longer comes from outside you because it pulses from the still point at your core.

Multi-Dimensional Intelligence reveals itself in this space in how you breathe, listen, and respond to life.

This is where the search becomes sovereignty. Where the seeker dissolves, and the field begins to respond to your frequency alone.

In the following pages, you'll activate the Pillars of Embodied multi-dimensional intelligence. These are living forces and frequencies that stabilize your multi-dimensional field and allow you to move through reality as a transmitter of coherence.

Each pillar is an aspect of your architecture and a core beam of your multi-dimensional template anchoring awareness, clarity, and creation through you.

This is embodiment as evolution, and this is how you walk as the field.

KEY QUESTIONS FOR EXPLORING
CHAPTER EIGHT

◊   In what ways are you embodying your multi-dimensional awareness in everyday life

◊   Which of the five archetypal pillars resonates most strongly with you at this moment, and which is inviting more of your attention?

◊   How can you bring greater coherence between your inner multi-dimensional awareness and the outer reality you are shaping?

Pillar One: The Seer Frequency

Perception Beyond the Human Firewall

Your journey begins with recalibrated perception and with the ability to see through the architecture of reality itself.

The Seer looks at the world differently.

Modern neurology confirms that while your conscious mind processes about 40 bits of data per second, your unconscious mind is sorting through over 11 million bits, selecting and prioritizing what will reach your awareness. Your waking life becomes a highlight reel curated by perceptual filters programmed through culture, trauma, and inherited memory. As Mihaly Csikszentmihalyi observed in his book *Flow*, attention shapes reality, and what you don't attend to doesn't exist for you.

Your senses are limitless, and they are a portal.

Beneath the noise of language, social signals, and input from the five senses, your biofield runs on a different kind of intelligence, a water-based architecture of sentience. Your body is over 70% water, yet this is not inert liquid. It is a living, responsive, and deeply intelligent crystalline recording system that shapes how you receive and transmit energy, information, and consciousness.

As shown in the work of Masaru Emoto, Veda Austin, and Dr. Gerald Pollack, water appears capable of holding structure, storing memory, and responding to frequency, thought, and intention. Emoto's frozen water crystals suggest that loving words create coherent geometries, whereas fear generates chaotic ones. Pollack's research reveals a fourth phase of water, the structured or exclusion zone (EZ) water that behaves more like a gel-like plasma, holds charge, and acts as a biological battery. Veda Austin's experiments show water organizing into symbolic forms in response to questions, hinting at a two-way communication between consciousness and the water within and around us.

Yet physics offers a different lens. When water freezes, it does not "print" a stored memory. It undergoes thermodynamic collapse. Liquid water, in its natural state, is the most dynamically restless substance known to biology, with hydrogen bonds breaking and reforming trillions of times per second. This is responsiveness, not archival storage. Freezing eliminates possibilities until only one lattice configuration survives. The beautiful glyphs in ice may be less a message from the past and more the final geometry that fit under constraint.

Perhaps both perspectives are valuable. While water may not "remember" it is exquisitely responsive, a modulator of energy, a synchronizer of biological systems, and an interface between matter and field.

Structured water refers to a highly ordered, coherent state. Unlike regular tap water or stagnant water, structured water forms hexagonal molecular arrangements that enhance cellular communication, conductivity, and vitality. In pranic states, fasting, or deep meditation, your body can produce endogenous water, pure, coherent, and untouched by external contaminants. This water is generated internally through metabolic and cellular processes, particularly during fat metabolism. This "living water" is not only clean and coherent but may carry a higher frequency untouched by external contaminants or emotional imprints. Some traditions and modern bioenergetic theories suggest that this endogenous water may be the true elixir and aligned with your original blueprint.

When your internal waters are clear and structured, your signal becomes coherent. You become less a storage vessel and more of a finely tuned antenna capable of receiving, transmitting, and harmonizing with higher frequencies of intelligence.

Multi-Dimensional Intelligence Practice: Frequency Field Command

1. Sense the Signature

Begin by scanning your body. Feel beneath surface emotion and notice the energetic texture of your field. Is it tense, expansive, elevated, or subdued? What quality is radiating from you?

2. Breathe the Frequency

Select a harmonic tone you wish to embody, perhaps stillness, clarity, joy, or trust. Breathe as if the air is calibrating every cell with that quality. Let the energy infuse your spine, skin, and space.

3. Encode Through Action

Let the frequency move outward through a gesture, a word, or the way you walk into a room. Subtle choices amplify the field. Frequency becomes structure when it is expressed with intention.

4. Observe the Field Response

Pay attention to how your environment shifts. Interactions, technology, and synchronicities all offer feedback. Your frequency is in dialogue with the world.

The Seer Frequency awakens when your nervous system becomes a scalar interface—a living antenna capable of perceiving energy while being embedded in the field. This goes beyond "intuition." It is a faculty of advanced consciousness, torsion field detection, timeline tracking, and light-body resonance reading.

Your heart, as measured by the HeartMath Institute, emits a magnetic field 60 times more powerful than the brain. It perceives events before they happen, because it operates at the zero-point axis (the still, coherent field of non-local awareness where potential collapses into form). Your heart is a constant transmitter, broadcasting electromagnetic signals into the environment. These signals influence others around you, whether consciously or not. In fact, studies show that when your heart is in a coherent state, it can synchronize the brainwaves and biorhythms of those nearby, a phenomenon known as social or energetic entrainment. Your inner state becomes a tuning fork for the collective field.

The Seer operates within a domain of deep pattern recognition where perception extends beyond appearances and begins to engage directly with the energetic frameworks that shape reality. From this space, the Seer becomes attuned to the organizing codes that hold form in place: the morphogenetic scaffolding that structures timelines, relationships, and events.

Real-World Example: Martín Prechtel – Keeper of the Seed Memory

Martín Prechtel, a Tz'utujil shaman and teacher, was trained in a remote Guatemalan village to perceive reality through the geometry of emotion, the color of dreams, and the feel of timelines stored in ancestral waters.

Multi-Dimensional Intelligence Practice: The Sensory Upgrade Protocol

1. Widen the Frame

Expand awareness three to six feet beyond your body. Your field is a sensory organ. Perceive with your skin, your gut, your spine.

2. Track the Tone

Sense the emotional temperature of a room. Is it spiking? Draining? Holding? Expanding? Practice naming the field, not telling the story.

3. Decode the Glitch

Listen not to words, but to waveform. Feel the incongruence when someone says, "I'm fine" but their field screams collapse.

4. Recalibrate Your Water

Sip structured water. Tone a vowel through your body. Breathe from the Central Axis. Re-center perception from the zero-point; not from your mind, but from the coherent signal at your core.

His role was to track the frequency of events before they happened. He could feel the grief in the village days before a death. He'd dream of the shift of seasons before the clouds gathered. He saw "memory stored in seeds, in rivers, in voices," and taught that all perception is communion with encoded fields if you're clear enough to receive.

Prechtel didn't learn this in books. He remembered it through the land, through fasting, through sacred sound, and through the coherence of water passed from elder to child.

In Multi-Dimensional Intelligence terms: he was living Seer frequency and reading time sideways. Reading water as language and reading the invisible architecture behind form.

Embodiment Shift: From Lens to Oracle

Seer Frequency refines your ability to receive reality without distortion and beyond the noise of thought, fear, or inherited programming. Rather than seeking answers, you begin to stabilize your presence, allowing subtle impressions to rise unfiltered through the field. Perception becomes precise, like a still pond reflecting truth without interference. In moments where others are overwhelmed by complexity, you remain anchored, attuned to the deeper signal beneath the surface. You read energy the way others read expressions, translating patterns into clarity. The Seer witnesses reality, and more than that, they engage with the blueprint behind it, subtly remapping the grid through embodied coherence.

Pillar Two: The Tuner Frequency

Frequency Mastery as Reality Architecture

Your body emits a signal long before you speak, decide, or act. It communicates in scalar waves, encoded with emotion, thought, memory, breath, and cellular resonance. That signal is your frequency acting as an architectural blueprint for your unfolding reality.

The Tuner Frequency is the embodiment of harmonic precision. It refines your ability to hold an energetic state with coherence, stability, and continuity.

You're no longer navigating life based on reaction or circumstance because you're shaping it from the inside out, tuning your internal field to broadcast alignment into the quantum fabric of space and time.

Every thought generates an electrical current, whereas emotions move with magnetic spin. These two forces combine to form scalar wave structures, which are complex, non-linear instruction sets that interact with the unified field. This interaction is what shapes the conditions you experience, the opportunities that emerge, and the direction your life begins to flow.

Peter Gariaev's Wave Genome Project demonstrated that DNA operates as a light-based communication system. It emits coherent photons and torsion fields that interact with the environment beyond the body. In this view, DNA becomes a dynamic transmitter receiving and projecting vibrational codes that align with your timeline trajectory and morphogenetic potential.

Frequency is the language your body uses to speak to the universe. It is formed through breath patterns, postural dynamics, hydration levels, emotional tone, and the coherence of your inner field. When these elements synchronize, the result is structural resonance and an energetic geometry that begins to shape and stabilize external outcomes.

At this level of embodiment, reality responds differently. Events begin to self-organize around your signal. People sense a field of clarity and calm around you. Environments become more fluid and cooperative, and you're no longer forcing outcomes or chasing alignment because you're radiating the pattern that life begins to mirror.

The Tuner is magnetic, becoming precise. Precision breeds entrainment and entrainment shifts form.

Real-World Example: Yildez – Dream Tracker of the Tuva Shamans (Siberia)

In the snow-covered regions of southern Siberia, the Tuva shamans speak of "sky singers" who attune to unseen frequencies to restore order. Yildez, one such elder, is known not for her words, but for her voice. During the ceremony, she chants familiar prayers or songs while listening to the field. She then releases a tone that emerges spontaneously, tuned to the dissonance in the space or person before her.

Her voice holds the frequency of coherence, reshaping timelines. Those present often experience emotional releases, vivid memories, or sudden insights. There is no explanation or analysis, she simply tunes the field until reality begins to reorganize.

Yildez's mastery lies in her ability to maintain frequency regardless of circumstances. Her body, breath, and voice become the instrument, and her presence is the practice.

This is Tuner Frequency in motion as she shapes the environment through the field she holds.

Multi-Dimensional Intelligence Practice: Frequency Field Command

1. Sense the Signature

Begin by scanning your body. Feel beneath surface emotion and notice the energetic texture of your field. Is it tense, expansive, elevated, or subdued? What quality is radiating from you?

2. Breathe the Frequency

Select a harmonic tone you wish to embody, perhaps stillness, clarity, joy, or trust. Breathe as if the air is calibrating every cell with that quality. Let the energy infuse your spine, skin, and space.

3. Encode Through Action

Let the frequency move outward through a gesture, a word, or the way you walk into a room. Subtle choices amplify the field. Frequency becomes structure when it is expressed with intention.

4. Observe the Field Response

Pay attention to how your environment shifts. Interactions, technology, and synchronicities all offer feedback. Your frequency is in dialogue with the world.

Embodiment Shift: Holding the Harmonic Blueprint

As the Tuner Frequency stabilizes within you, your field begins to emit a consistent harmonic that informs your environment. This coherence becomes perceptible to others, shaping the tone of interactions, the outcomes of events, and the atmosphere of the spaces you inhabit.

Energy starts to self-organize around the patterns you hold. Conversations flow with greater ease. Choices feel naturally aligned. Timelines unfold with less resistance because your internal architecture provides a stable point of reference.

Frequency mastery is a state of attuned presence. From this place, you begin to build new realities through the clarity of what you transmit. Structure forms around resonance, and movement follows the rhythm you sustain.

This is the essence of tuning: a living signal that composes the future in real time.

Pillar Three: The Navigator Frequency

Timeline Alignment and Quantum Movement

Navigation begins with resonance and a felt sense of alignment that emerges before any conscious decision is made. Every choice is preceded by a subtle shift, and every shift is initiated by a signal or impulse arising from deeper within your field. Beneath that signal lies orientation: your innate capacity to sense where you are in relation to your highest potential, your energetic landscape, and the multi-dimensional map that is already unfolding through you.

The Navigator Frequency sharpens your orientation within the multi-dimensional field, and develops a refined sensitivity to movement when energy calls for forward motion, stillness, or redirection. This intelligence emerges from coherence with your inner compass, guided by the subtle pull of trajectories already resonant with your field. Navigation becomes an act of resonance and attunement to the energetic geometry of unfolding possibilities before they materialize into form.

Every possibility exists as a pattern. These patterns carry tone, density, momentum, and emotional signature. They can be felt. They can be read. And they can be selected through attunement.

The moment you choose with coherence, a new trajectory takes shape. Each thought, gesture, or decision contributes to a ripple effect that weaves into the geometry of your life. The Navigator becomes sensitive to these inflection points, recognizing moments as portals into alternate sequences of reality.

This is a different kind of intelligence. It's less concerned with control and more attuned to convergence and how people, places, and timing coalesce when the field is aligned.

Over time, the body becomes the compass. The field becomes the instrument. And the signal that rises through you becomes the guide.

Real-World Example: Tiokasin Ghosthorse – Lakota Wisdom Keeper of the Language of the Land

Tiokasin Ghosthorse, a Lakota elder and teacher of the Cheyenne River Lakota Nation, shares a way of moving through the world that is deeply anchored in energetic listening. His teachings often focus on relational awareness with people, but also with rivers, trees, winds, and stones.

In his tradition, direction arises through communion. One does not decide where to go; one listens to where one is being called. In his words: "Language is used to be in relationship with the world."

When Tiokasin moves through a landscape, he feels its song. He senses when to remain, when to turn, and when to speak. His navigation is guided by field coherence, tracking the resonance between body, Earth, and spirit. He is a reminder that timelines are living rivers, and you can feel their current in the present moment.

This is the essence of the Navigator Frequency: living in harmony with unfolding intelligence and responding from within it.

Multi-Dimensional Intelligence Practice: Timeline Alignment Protocol

1. Return to the Central Axis

Close your eyes and bring awareness to the Central Axis point. Breathe into this center until your energy stabilizes. Feel yourself as the still-point within motion.

2. Sense the Field of Potentials

From this centered place, invite three versions of the same decision or path into awareness. Each one carries a tone, texture, and sensation. Explore them through the body, not the mind.

3. Feel for Alignment

Notice which path feels fluid, expansive, and synchronously charged. Observe your breath, posture, and heart rhythm as each timeline is explored. These physiological cues are data points.

4. Choose and Commit

Once alignment is clear, allow that path to fully rise within you. Imagine stepping into it, not as imagination, but as a living frequency becoming form. Take one action that harmonizes with this field.

Embodiment Shift: Orienting from the Inner Compass

As the Navigator Frequency becomes stable, movement arises from inner clarity. Each step carries more precision. Patterns of indecision begin to dissolve, replaced by subtle yet distinct guidance that comes from coherence, not effort.

Choices no longer require mental verification, and you begin to feel the shape of your life from the inside out. The path ahead opens when you hold resonance with it and when your energy aligns with the architecture of what is already waiting.

This is the mastery of moving with the unfolding geometry of your own becoming.

Pillar Four: The Transmitter Frequency

Living as Signal

Every cell emits light. Every breath shapes the field. You are transmitting even when silent.

The Transmitter Frequency emerges when coherence is sustained long enough for the body to become a stabilized conduit for Source current. This is a harmonic presence that builds itself through clarity, resonance, and continuous inner alignment.

Transmission is the natural consequence of embodied frequency. When the physical, emotional, and energetic systems are synchronized, your presence begins to imprint the field around you. Your voice takes on an organizing quality. Your gestures and even your stillness become carriers of encoded information.

Transmission emerges when the field becomes internally ordered and spacious enough to carry signal. As the body stabilizes into coherence, it begins to express a deeper intelligence that precedes words and exists beneath personality. Communication shifts from explanation to resonance. Each expression carries the memory of wholeness, encoded in tone, rhythm, and energetic precision.

In this state, presence becomes impactful in ways that extend beyond intention. Others may feel a subtle recalibration, a slowing of breath, or an unexpected return to clarity simply by being near you. Your system emits coherence, and that coherence becomes an invitation. The body becomes an instrument of organization, holding a frequency that aligns the space, the moment, and the collective field.

To embody the Transmitter Frequency is to move as living resonance, expressing from the crystalline strata of the DNA, from the Central Axis gate, and from the still-point node that remembers the pattern of wholeness before fragmentation occurred.

Real-World Example: Uncle Bob Randall – Aboriginal Custodian of the Uluru Field

Uncle Bob Randall, an Anangu elder of the Yankunytjatjara people and a traditional custodian of Uluru, rarely offered long explanations or abstract teachings. He was known for simply being in resonance with the land. Visitors who sat with him would often feel spontaneous waves of stillness, tears, or deep release without any words exchanged.

Multi-Dimensional Practice: Scalar Breath & Tonal Field Activation

1. Scalar Convergence

BreathingVisualize your body at the center of a six-pointed star (above, below, front, back, left, right). Inhale from all six directions simultaneously into the Central Axis point (between heart and throat). Let this breath converge into stillness at the center. (This builds on the six-pointed breath introduced in Chapter Six for Central Axis Synchronization, now expanded with sound to deepen resonance.)

2. Activate the Transmitter Field with Tone

On the exhale, softly vocalize a harmonic tone: Eyaa, Uhm, Aah, Urh, or Ka. Let the sound vibrate through your spine and radiate from the chest. Repeat until you feel the resonance stabilize into your body and auric field.

3. Encode the Field with Feeling-Tone

Select a core essence to transmit, such as peace, remembrance, reverence, or unity. Infuse this essence into your tone and allow the transmission to ripple outward without needing to direct it.

4. Anchor the Light Signature

Place your hands gently over the Central Axis point. Sense the subtle magnetic field around your chest expand. Stay here until the tone dissolves into silence, allowing the encoded transmission to anchor fully.

This activation stabilizes your morphogenetic field and strengthens your ability to communicate through harmonic presence.

His presence transmitted the Dreaming. It didn't need to be taught; it entered through the body. He held the frequency of place, of ancestors, and of truth embedded in the red soil. When he spoke, it was slow, spacious, rhythmic; each word felt as if it had come from deep time.

Transmission unfolded through continuity as an unbroken connection between presence and field. Through his resonance, others remembered something essential that lived quietly within them, waiting to be recognized.

Embodiment Shift: Presence as Instruction

The Transmitter Frequency expresses through the quiet stability of a coherent field. At this level, your presence becomes an architecture through which higher-order intelligence flows subtly, grounded, and deeply instructive. There is no need to push energy outward or search for the right moment to speak because your field already carries the memory of alignment, and that memory begins to organize the space around you.

When your breath, tone, and movement are informed by resonance, others begin to shift without knowing why. The nervous system entrains coherence before it interprets meaning. Words become optional. Movement becomes encoded. You're broadcasting from pattern.

Transmission arises when your field becomes so clear and structured that distortion has no place to anchor. Every step becomes a calibration. Every silence carries a signal. You begin to move through the world as an open source of alignment available to those ready to remember.

This is intelligence in form, held in the breath. Radiating through the skin. Anchored in stillness. Transmitting the frequency of truth without distortion.

Pillar Five: The Architect Frequency

Building Reality through Conscious Design and Grid Intelligence

Everything emits structure. Even silence has scaffolding.

The Architect Frequency is your capacity to create coherence on behalf of the whole and to design timelines, spaces, businesses, systems, and cultures that reflect the intelligence of your multi-dimensional self. You are expressing a frequency as well as constructing with it.

The Architect Frequency brings form to vision.

It invites you to participate in the unseen infrastructure that shapes how energy flows, decisions ripple, and experiences crystallize into reality. While others may feel the field or navigate possibilities, the Architect gives structure to them through design, rhythm, and coherence.

This pillar activates when you begin to engage consciously with the patterns behind what appears. You recognize that everything you create sits within a living grid, whether that's a business, a conversation, a social community, or a physical space. The grid holds intention, resonance, memory, and trajectory. Through refinement of your awareness, you begin to sense how those structures carry influence far beyond the moment of their construction.

Your frequency becomes the framework informing how things unfold and how long they last.

The Architect listens for the underlying resonance in systems and environments. You start to notice where a plan lacks integrity, where a team or message begins to fracture, or where alignment is missing in an otherwise effective structure. These signals reveal themselves through subtle feedback, whether through tension in communication, recurring disruptions, or unexpected energy drains.

In these moments, your capacity is about more than simply fixing. It's about refining the frequency architecture to restore flow.

Morphogenetic fields, the blueprint fields that guide development in living systems, respond to coherence. When intention, energy, and form are synchronized, those fields strengthen and hold shape. The Architect learns to align with these natural currents, weaving new structures into the collective that support regeneration, clarity, and expansion.

This work happens through design. Through language. Through process. Through space. You begin to place frequency into form, shaping energetic blueprints that others can live within.

Real-World Example: Clare Graves & Spiral Dynamics

In the 1970s, psychologist Clare W. Graves introduced a model of human development that does not unfold in a straight, step-by-step progression, but rather through successive layers or waves of consciousness. Later refined into Spiral Dynamics, this model illustrates how individuals, organizations, and cultures move through frequency-based stages, each one reflecting a distinct worldview, value system, and reality structure.

Graves observed psychology and then architected a map for how consciousness evolves through systems.

Today, Spiral Dynamics is used to redesign governments, companies, and global negotiations. It helps leaders build for the future, not just repair the past. This is the Architect Frequency in action, perceiving the pattern underneath the pattern, and creating frameworks that harmonize with higher-order truth.

Multi-Dimensional Practice: The Reality Grid Calibration Protocol

1. Tune into the Structure

Select a living container. This might be a project, relationship, business model, offering, or environment. Bring awareness to its underlying energetic pattern. Ask: what frequency holds this in place?

2. Sense the Grid Distortions

Notice where energy becomes erratic, where clarity drops, or where loops of mis-alignment repeat. Let your awareness soften as you feel into these tension points. What is being signaled?

3. Apply Harmonic Design

Visualize the entire system infused with a specific harmonic quality, such as simplicity, elegance, sovereignty, or truth. Feel this resonance radiating from your field into the grid. Allow it to reshape the design energetically.

4. Translate into Form

Take a clear action to embed that new harmonic into the container: restructure a step, edit a message, shift a boundary, or create something new. Coherence becomes durable when frequency is anchored into material choices.

While you may never design political systems, your words, your offers, your content, your conversations are all grids. You are always building.

The question is: *Are you building from habit or from harmonic precision?*

Embodiment Shift: Holding Design as Intelligence

The Architect creates the conditions through which clarity can emerge.

You begin to recognize yourself as a stabilizing force and someone who can hold the pulse of a future potential, guiding it into form without distorting its essence. Everything you create carries a signature, and that signature becomes a signal that organizes reality.

In this field, design is presence and your leadership flows through alignment. Your work becomes a living architecture that supports coherence for others.

You are shaping the what, how, when, and why of evolution.

Your frequency leaves an imprint. Your creations hold code, and every structure you build becomes part of the grid the future will walk upon.

Multi-Dimensional Embodiment Activation

Stabilizing Your Multi-Dimensional Architecture

Each frequency you've encountered from awareness, resonance, navigation, transmission, and design reveals a distinct layer of your multi-dimensional intelligence. These are living patterns encoded into your energy field, guiding how you engage with reality, organize timelines, and influence form through presence.

This activation brings those layers into synchronized alignment. Your breath becomes a stabilizing force. Your posture holds signal. Your field emits coherence that reorganizes space and interaction. Through this calibration, your system begins to function as a unified architecture anchoring the intelligence of Source into matter, moment by moment.

Return to this practice whenever refinement, clarity, or realignment is called for. Each time you engage with it, the grid of your being becomes more luminous, more structured, and more capable of transmitting precision into the quantum field.

You are the design, the interface, and the field in motion.

Archetype	Core Function	Key Traits	Practices for Embodiment
Seer	Expanded perception	Clairvoyance, intuitive insight, multi-dimensional awareness	Pineal activation, sensory expansion exercises, extra-ocular vision
Tuner	Energetic mastery	Frequency alignment, coherence creation, emotional regulation	Heart-brain coherence, sound & frequency work, breath mastery
Navigator	Timeline awareness	Quantum decision-making, sensing probability shifts, fluidity in time	Timeline mapping, lucid dreaming, quantum jumping
Transmitter	Coherent influence	Broadcasting stable frequencies, radiating zero-point presence, field imprinting	Embodied resonance, presence practices, intention transmission
Architect	Conscious creation	Manifestation from zero-point, blueprint activation, intentional design	Visioning, field imprinting, morphogenetic coding

Step 1: Anchor the Seer

Bring awareness into the space around your body. Expand your sensing 360 degrees. Let your skin dissolve into light. Begin perceiving the subtle field:

» What are you aware of beyond words?

» What tone does the moment carry?

Affirmation:

I see from the field. I perceive beyond the veil.

Step 2: Stabilize the Tuner

Breathe deeply through your nose and into the Central Axis point. Let the breath calibrate your field.

Choose the frequency you wish to hold, such as clarity, depth, stillness or joy, and feel it radiating outward.

Affirmation:

My frequency is clean. My coherence leads.

Step 3: Activate the Navigator

Close your eyes and feel into your current timeline, sensing which direction pulls your energy forward. Now call forth the version of you who already holds the highest outcome and merge with their posture, their presence, their breath.

Affirmation:

I move with precision. I align with my future self.

Step 4: Amplify the Transmitter

Let your body become luminous by visualizing light emanating from your DNA, your voice, and your cells. Speak aloud a tone or truth that carries your current signal into the quantum web.

Affirmation:

I am the field in motion. My presence carries intelligence.

Step 5: Construct with the Architect

Bring attention to a space, structure, or intention you are currently creating, such as a business, family, offering, or community. Scan it as a grid. Where is harmony? Where is noise?

Now breathe an upgraded blueprint into it and anchor the design.

Affirmation:

I build in alignment. I structure with Source.

Completion: Embodied Multi-Dimensional Intelligence

Place your hands over your chest or Central Axis point and feel all five frequencies resonating through you as a living architecture.

You are the Seer.

You are the Tuner.

You are the Navigator.

You are the Transmitter.

You are the Architect.

You walk as a stabilizing node in the field, re-organizing distortion, and as the embodiment of Multi-Dimensional Intelligence in motion.

Matrix Human	Multi-Dimensional Intelligent Embodied Human
Reacts from past programming	Responds from present coherence
Seeks external validation	Follows internal frequency
Plans life linearly	Navigates timelines fluidly
Identifies with role or story	Lives as a multi-dimensional field
Consumes information	Transmits resonance
Driven by fear, duty, or habit	Guided by alignment and intuition
Caught in polarity and reactivity	Anchored in presence and paradox
Sees life as happening *to* them	Co-creates reality through conscious energy

This table is here to create clarity, and you may find yourself somewhere in between. You may have already glimpsed your Multi-Dimensional Intelligence embodiment through moments of profound clarity, instant knowing, energetic calibration, or previews of your future self.

INTEGRATION KEYS
Living as a Multi-Dimensional Human

- Multi-Dimensional Intelligence is something to re-member. This journey has activated dormant codes, sharpened perception, and restored access to the deeper architecture of who you are.

- You are the signal, the stabilizer, and the source. As you walk through the world, your field carries a frequency that informs others, re-patterns environments, and reminds the collective of its multi-dimensional nature.

- Every practice, insight, and revelation in this book points to embodiment. Multi-Dimensional Intelligence is about amplification of presence, expansion of choice, and mastery of movement across timelines, states, and systems.

- Multi-Dimensional Intelligence is a convergence point. You carry the original codes. You hold the inner technology. You are the future, arriving fully now.

Are You Activating Multi-Dimensional Intelligence?
A Self-Scan for Embodied Multi-Dimensional Intelligence

Multi-Dimensional Intelligence is something you embody. These self-reflection prompts are designed to tune your awareness to the subtle signals, choices, and capacities of an awakened multi-dimensional field. There are no right or wrong answers, simply resonance. As you read them, feel into your body. Let the questions scan your field.

1. Can you discern when a thought is truly yours vs. a broadcast from collective programming?

2. Do you sense shifts or distortions in a space before anything is said or seen?

3. Are your decisions guided by a felt resonance, even when logic disagrees?

4. Do you recognize nonlinear time through synchronicity, déjà vu, or layered timelines?

5. Can you feel the difference between mind-driven goals and soul-aligned impulses?

6. Do you experience moments of knowing without knowing how you know?

7. Are you able to shift your frequency consciously to enter clarity, calm, or creative flow?

The more these questions evoke a felt response in you, the more you are living from your Multi-Dimensional Intelligence.

A Final Transmission: Becoming the Living Field

Many years ago, during a pivotal chapter of my life, I found myself seeking peace in unfamiliar places. I was invited into the gentle company of the Brahma Kumaris, a spiritual organization rooted in Raja Yoga meditation. They hold a vision of time as a 5,000-year cycle, endlessly repeating, where everything that has been will come again. In their presence, I felt only stillness, simplicity, acceptance, and kindness.

At one of their larger gatherings in London, a few of their dignified spiritual elders were seated at the front offering *drishti*. This is a form of subtle transmission where the eyes become conduits of silent blessing. With my head lowered and my eyes resting softly on the floor, I felt the moment her gaze found me. I didn't look up. I didn't need to. A wave of energy moved through me so tangibly, it shifted something beyond words. Decades later, I still remember the exact texture of that moment.

This is the power of coherence. The power of presence. The ability to hold a field so clear, so attuned, that others feel nourished by your being without a single word spoken.

People often tell me, *"There's something about your energy."* That is the feedback I trust. It tells me my field is clear. My signal is stable.

Another mentor once shared that he could sense illness and misalignments in others with startling clarity. At first, he tried to help directly but found that most people resisted unsolicited insight. So, he stopped offering words. Instead, he walked through the world with a quiet presence, knowing that his coherent field could nudge a pattern back into alignment. Sometimes the person might later choose to seek help, without ever knowing why. That is subtle influence. Not through force, but through frequency.

Of course, this is not about saving others or overriding their choices. It is about remembering your capacity to transmit harmony, simply by being it.

There comes a moment in every true journey when the seeker becomes the signal. When the tools fall away, and what remains is not what you've learned, it is who you've become.

This is that moment.

Multi-Dimensional Intelligence is a frequency already embedded within you, waiting for your readiness to remember.

This is where you become the **Seer**, the **Tuner**, the **Navigator**, the **Architect**, the **Transmitter**. You are not waiting for a shift because you are the shift, embodying the frequency that catalyzes it.

- Can you imagine walking into a room and stabilizing the entire field through your presence alone?
- Can you imagine sensing a timeline split and choosing the one that unlocks your next evolution?
- Can you imagine becoming so attuned to Source that your very breath carries instruction to the grid?

More than a student of Multi-Dimensional Intelligence, you are the living architecture of it. The DNA carrier. The field stabilizer. The one who pulses coherence into the collective just by existing in alignment.

As the world rushes toward artificial intelligence, you embody Multi-Dimensional Intelligence. As systems fragment, you hold the original code, and as many seek safety in simulation, you radiate a frequency that reminds others of who they truly are.

» You are here to transmit coherence so others awaken to themselves.
» You are here to out-frequency distortion and walk the new timeline with clarity.
» You are here to embody what others have forgotten is possible.

The future of Multi-Dimensional Intelligence is already alive in you, in your silence, your precision, your choices and your way of being. It is in how you love, how you stand, how you enter the moment without flinching.

The next stage of human evolution is a return to your original design.

The wild, wondrous, multi-dimensional odyssey begins now.

You are the blueprint. You are the bridge. You are the beginning.

You searched the sky for signs and stars,
Mapped the mind, remembered Mars.
You cracked the code, undid the spin,
Forgot the door was always within.
You touched the edge of thought and form,
Let silence split the perfect storm.
You drank the dark, became the flame,
And left behind the need for name.
You tuned your bones to unseen sound,
Felt timelines ripple underground.
The future folded in your chest,
A pulse of knowing, deeply blessed.
You spoke in tones the soul could hear,
Rewrote the grid through love, not fear.
You held the line when others slept,
You wept the codes the cosmos kept.
Now you are not what came before.
You are not seeker, wound, or war.
You are the breath between the stars,
The field, the flame, the Avatar.
You are the stillness in the shift,
The light that doesn't need to lift.
The one who walks, yet leaves no trace,
Except a song, a sacred space.
No longer waiting to begin,
You were always the frequency within.

AFTERWORD

Following the groundbreaking work in her last two books, *Re-Imagine You: BioRegenesis of the DNA Blueprint through Source Feeding*, and *YOU the Divine Genius*, Dr. Carol Talbot returns with her most potent transmission yet. If we have the faith and courage to follow the path she herself has walked, we'll find ourselves even closer to a fuller revelation of ourselves and our place in a vast cosmos.

This body of work offers golden threads to guide us home to our highest remembrance.

In a world where so many have forgotten their place in the cosmos, Dr. Carol reminds us that we are encoded with unfathomable potential. Consider the energy released by the splitting of a single atom and then reflect on the 450 trillion cells within your body, each one holding a holographic blueprint of consciousness and creation. You are a living library of light!

This book reads like a charm and as an activator. It is a living document encoded with resonance. In an age dulled by reductive models of intelligence and a numbing of the senses, Dr. Carol restores the true magic of multi-dimensional intelligence, emergent complexity, and deep inner technology.

She weaves together quantum science, frequency archetypes, and even the elusive Dicyanin dye, a window into veiled realities once reserved for the initiated. What once seemed disparate is revealed as coherent. This goes beyond presenting models; this is memory activation.

Dr. Carol reminds us that the brain is not the origin of consciousness but a receiver, and that complexity, far from being chaotic, often conceals a higher order. Yet she does not leave us suspended in abstraction. The icing on this layered cake of revelation are the *Five Pillars of Radiant Architecture* and the *Integration Keys* at the end of each chapter. These gift us with tuning forks for alignment and illuminate the concepts she explores. Each one invites application, embodiment, and revelation.

Some may find her insights bold. Others, deeply familiar, as if remembered from another place or time. For those willing to see beyond consensus reality, this book isn't just read. It's experienced.

Dr. Carol, like Lewis Carroll, invites us through the veil to participate. Having come this far, you now stand at a threshold, and the real work begins.

Welcome to the dance.

Phil Gruber

REFERENCES & RESOURCES

Books & Published Research

- Braden, Gregg. *The Divine Matrix: Bridging Time, Space, Miracles, and Belief.* Hay House, 2007.

- Burr, Harold Saxton. *The Fields of Life: Our Links with the Universe.* Ballantine, 1973.CH

- Castaneda, Carlos. *The Teachings of Don Juan: A Yaqui Way of Knowledge.* University of California Press, 1968.

- Emoto, Masaru. *The Hidden Messages in Water.* Atria Books, 2004.

- Libet, Benjamin. "Unconscious cerebral initiative and the role of conscious will in voluntary action." *Behavioral and Brain Sciences* 8.4 (1985): 529-539.

- McTaggart, Lynne. *The Field: The Quest for the Secret Force of the Universe.* HarperCollins, 2008.

- Radin, Dean. *The Conscious Universe: The Scientific Truth of Psychic Phenomena.* HarperOne, 1997.

- Rein, Glen. "The Biochemical and Biological Effects of Human Intentions." *Subtle Energies & Energy Medicine Journal*, 1992.

- Rupert Sheldrake. *The Presence of the Past: Morphic Resonance and the Habits of Nature.* Park Street Press, 1995.

- Talbot, Michael. *The Holographic Universe.* HarperPerennial, 1992.

- Varela, Francisco, Thompson, Evan, and Rosch, Eleanor. *The Embodied Mind: Cognitive Science and Human Experience.* MIT Press, 1991.

- Wadhams, Peter. *A Farewell to Ice: A Report from the Arctic.* Oxford University Press, 2016.

- Winter, Dan. *DNA as a Wave:* Online research and videos via www.fractalfield.com.

- Sarfarazi, Mohsen Paul. *Consciousness Revisited* and related works. Available online.

Scientific & Technical Concepts Cited

- Quantum Superposition and Observer Effect (referencing Schrödinger's Cat, Heisenberg's Uncertainty Principle)

- HeartMath Institute Research on Cardiac Coherence and the Electromagnetic Field of the Heart www.heartmath.org

- Phantom DNA Effect – Gariaev, P.P., "Wave-based genetic information transmission."

- Cymatics and Frequency Patterning (Hans Jenny)

- Water Memory and Structured Water Studies (Luc Montagnier, Gerald Pollack)

Key Websites & Independent Research Portals

- HeartMath Institute
- Institute of Noetic Sciences
- Rupert Sheldrake's Research
- Veda Austin – The Secret Intelligence of Water
- Dan Winter – Fractal Field & DNA Physics
- Cynthia Sue Larson – Reality Shifts

Suggested Reading for Further Exploration

- Baird T. Spalding, *The Life and Teachings of the Masters of the Far East*
- Jean Houston, *The Possible Human*
- Amit Goswami, *The Self-Aware Universe*
- David Bohm, *Wholeness and the Implicate Order*
- Thomas Campbell, *My Big TOE (Theory of Everything)*

GLOSSARY OF TERMS

Amnesia Fields

Energetic distortions or artificial grids that block access to soul memory and higher awareness. They act like veils, suppressing multi-dimensional perception and causing forgetfulness of your greater identity and mission.

Bio-Spiritual Regenesis/Bioregenesis

The process of repairing and restoring the original divine template of human DNA to its highest frequency potential. Involves physical, emotional, mental, and spiritual detox and integration of Source frequencies.

Consciousness Kernel

A core informational unit or identity field within you that contains the blueprint of your soul's essence, purpose, and multi-dimensional data. It functions like a seed or central code of your unique expression.

Diamond Sun DNA Template

An advanced multi-dimensional DNA configuration composed of 12 or more strands, each corresponding to different dimensions of consciousness. Represents the full embodiment of Source consciousness through the human form.

Distortions (DNA / Perception)

Artificial frequency interferences that disrupt the flow of Source consciousness through your system. They can manifest as belief systems, trauma, environmental toxins, or inherited programming that block your original blueprint.

Endogenous Water

Structured, living water generated within your body during deep states of fasting, cellular purification, or heightened energetic alignment. It differs from external (exogenous) water by being crystalline, coherent, and life-enhancing.

Energy Coherence

A state of internal harmony and alignment where your physical, emotional, mental, and energetic fields operate in resonance with your higher self and Source. Essential for stabilizing multi-dimensional awareness.

Fractal Antenna (DNA)

The concept that DNA functions as a receiver and transmitter of frequency-based information across dimensions, similar to a fractal antenna that picks up non-local energy signatures.

Frequency Architecture

The internal blueprint of how your multi-dimensional energy systems are structured. It governs your perception, timeline orientation, DNA expression, and capacity to interface with reality.

Higher Sensory Perception (HSP)

Abilities that extend beyond the five physical senses, such as telepathy, clairvoyance, extra-ocular vision, or precognition. These are considered latent capacities of activated DNA.

Liquid Crystal Superconductors (DNA)

A view of DNA as a dynamic, intelligent medium that conducts energy and information like a liquid crystal, supporting quantum-level communication between cells and higher dimensional fields.

Multi-Dimensional Intelligence

A framework for perceiving, interpreting, and operating from your multi-dimensional nature. Unlike IQ or EQ, Multi-Dimensional Intelligence reflects your ability to navigate energy, time, frequency, and consciousness as a coherent whole.

Morphogenetic Field

An energetic blueprint field that stores patterns, structures, and instructions for the formation of all biological life and consciousness systems. Coined by Rupert Sheldrake and further expanded in Quantum Morphogenetic Science.

Phantom DNA Effect

A phenomenon where the energetic imprint of DNA remains in a vacuum even after the physical DNA has been removed, indicating a field-based or morphic presence of genetic memory.

Quantum Jumping / Timeline Navigation

The conscious shifting between parallel timelines or versions of self by altering your frequency, choices, or perception. Based on the idea that all potentials exist simultaneously in a quantum field.

Signal Consciousness

The intelligence of your energetic system that operates beneath thoughts and identity. This signal interfaces with the quantum field, guides timeline movement, and responds to coherence or dissonance.

Source Feeding

A form of nourishment not dependent on physical food but on pranic, photonic, or frequency-based energy. Sometimes associated with breatharianism or living on light, this state reflects DNA regeneration and alignment with Source.

Structured Water

Highly ordered water that forms crystalline, hexagonal molecular arrangements. Structured water is said to hold memory, respond to intention, and enhance cellular communication.

Timeline Collapse

The merging or dissolution of parallel or probable timelines, often triggered by significant shifts in frequency, awareness, or collective consciousness. Can result in sudden life changes or quantum leaps.

Torsion Fields

Spiral, scalar energy fields believed to propagate faster than light and capable of carrying information. They are seen as the medium for consciousness transfer, non-local communication, and energetic memory.

Zero Point Field

A field of pure potential and stillness that underlies all creation. It is considered the meeting point between matter and consciousness, and a gateway to Source intelligence.

ABOUT THE AUTHOR

Dr. Carol Talbot is a visionary voice in the evolution of human consciousness. As the creator of *Multi-Dimensional Intelligence*, she offers a transmission and an invitation to remember who you truly are beneath the layers of programming and perceived limitation. Her words do more than teach; they initiate.

With a PhD in Quantum Morphogenetic Science, Dr. Carol is internationally recognized for her groundbreaking work on DNA bioregenesis, Source Feeding, and consciousness expansion. Her research reveals that intelligence is not confined to the brain or emotions; it is a multi-dimensional architecture encoded into your very being. She teaches that when you align your field, your frequency, and your form, you awaken the dormant codes that hold your most extraordinary potential.

Founder of *The Possibility Hub*, Dr. Carol is a master catalyst for transformation, known for her ability to distill complex esoteric and scientific concepts into practical, embodied wisdom. Her global work spans retreats, keynotes, firewalks, and private mentoring, each designed to activate rapid realignment and inner mastery.

Drawing from decades of experience in neuro-linguistic programming, energy medicine, sound, breath, and subtle anatomy, she blends original technologies with cutting-edge science to help others become conscious creators of their own reality. Her transmission is clear: You are the interface between dimensions. You are the navigator of timelines. You are the signal the world has been waiting for.

Her bestselling books, including *YOU the Divine Genius* and *Re-Imagine You*, have inspired thousands to detox physically, mentally, emotionally, and spiritually, liberating themselves from the matrix of conditioning and reclaiming their multi-dimensional design. With *Multi-Dimensional Intelligence*, Dr. Carol now offers a blueprint for navigating the future of human evolution.

Whether through her speaking, writing, or mentoring, Dr. Carol Talbot opens gateways into expanded perception, quantum creation, and embodied mastery. Her work is not about improving the self; it is about activating the *truth* of who you already are.

Because this isn't just personal development.

This is a dimensional awakening.

www.ingramcontent.com/pod-product-compliance
Lightning Source LLC
Chambersburg PA
CBHW071953090426
42740CB00011B/1921